LINSEED AND FISHPASTE

The winter before last Mark Bussell clocked up 2,400 miles on a moped in a single week visiting every first-class cricket ground in the country. He has toured Belgium with his puppet theatre show based on the 1932–33 'Bodyline' series and recently challenged Ray Illingworth to a 24-hour non-stop flamenco contest. But life is not always this solemn; he is co-editor of the cricket magazine *The Googly*, and some days he finds time to be a TV writer and producer.

4970

Linseed and Fishpaste

Confessions of a Cricket Nut

Mark Bussell

HEADLINE

First published in 1997
by HEADLINE BOOK PUBLISHING

First published in paperback in 1998
by HEADLINE BOOK PUBLISHING

10 9 8 7 6 5 4 3 2 1

ISBN 0 7472 5729 9

Printed and bound in Great Britain by
Mackays of Chatham PLC, Chatham, Kent

HEADLINE BOOK PUBLISHING
A division of Hodder Headline PLC
338 Euston Road
London NW1 3BH

CONTENTS

ACKNOWLEDGEMENTS

I'd like to thank Ian Marshall at Headline for his encouragement and support; Justin Sbresni who has traded half-baked theories with me about the inadequacies of the England cricket team for over a decade now; Dave, Matt, and Nigel for arranging all those waistline-defying encounters with other sad blokes on Sundays; and most of all Fran who lets me watch as much cricket as I do.

INTRODUCTION

I once heard it argued that if Martians landed on Earth and they wanted by a single question to differentiate the British from the rest of the peoples of the planet, the question to ask would be: who is Valerie Singleton?

But what if instead they wanted to isolate a subset of that group – genuine cricket fans? Not the people who still make jokes about googlies or still find funny that tea towel that explains the rules of cricket (you know, when he's in, he's out etc.), nor even the vast majority of people who follow the ups but mainly downs of the England cricket team, catch the highlights occasionally on the box, and maybe every now and then are persuaded to join their mates and dress up as Mr Blobby at a Test match in the hope of catching themselves on the highlights. No, I mean the real cricket fan. In fact, the people who can answer correctly the question: who is Jim Foat? This book is first and foremost for them.

Not long ago, I took my girlfriend's godson, nine-year-old Mark, to see his first game of first-class cricket – Surrey v Gloucestershire at The Oval (or The Foster's Oval as the marketing men there would have it). I have to confess to some deep primeval feeling during this event. This was a rite of passage: man and boy; boy and man. Leaving the womenfolk behind and going off together to usher in the early stages of manhood. In another society we'd be going off into the middle of the forest. I'd do something nasty to his genitalia with an old knife, give him a dock leaf to wipe away the blood, and abandon him. He'd then have to mince back to the village, clutching what was left of his manhood, without being mauled to death by a lion. Luckily for both of us, but particularly for Mark, all we had to do was entertain ourselves until Mark's mother came back from Ikea.

So there we were sitting in the famous old pavilion with me doing my utmost to 'sell' cricket to him. I regaled him with history – Hutton's 364, Bradman's duck denying him a career Test average of over 100, spectators mopping up puddles on the pitch to allow play to restart and Deadly Derek Underwood skittle the Aussies, and Devon's nine for 57. I gave him the full tour of the ground – the long room, the indoor cricket school, the library, bombarding him with trivia like The Oval having the largest playing area in the country and the most sophisticated electronic scoreboard. But he was not impressed. I bought him a Foster's scorecard and a Foster's cola, followed by a Foster's Mars Bar, another Foster's cola, and a Surrey sunhat to keep out the drizzle and all I got was: where is the crowd? Why is everyone watching so old? Why don't the players wear coloured kit? Why do they keep coming off? Why are we watching six men in luminous anoraks wheel three large white skateboards on to the pitch every ten minutes? Where can we get a hot dog? When can we go home?

I tried everything to instil in this young mind the joy of cricket – I even got him Dean Hodgson's autograph for Christ's sake! But it was all to no avail. For some reason this small moment in his life was not laden with the same meaning as that day long ago in 1973 when I got Jim Foat's scribble. Mark was not seduced by the studied languidness, the solace of statistics and trivia, the glorious utter pointlessness of it all. For if all sport is ultimately pointless, cricket positively revels in its pointlessness, taking anything up to five days (though more likely three if England are involved) to reach its pointless conclusion.

For a moment or two I came over all *Daily Telegraph* leader page and inwardly berated the youth of today, impugning their usefulness and decrying their values: a whole generation had grown up who'd rather watch Sonic the Hedgehog than . . . well, Darren Bicknell! But then the doubts. Oh God! Maybe it's me? Maybe I was the one out of step? Perhaps Mark was right. Maybe this *was* an absurd – not to say 'sad' (to use the modern vernacular) – little world. But then the umpires walked out to a ripple of applause followed by the shambling rabble of players and Darren Bicknell snicked Kevin Cooper's first ball past slip and down to the Vauxhall End for four where it got trapped under the covers. A wait of some three or four minutes ensued as an assortment of groundsmen and players tried to retrieve it. I looked around at our fellow spectators: a handful of pensioners and a man wearing a tam-o'-shanter who looked an unfortunate indictment of the previous government's care in the community programme. Another man with his flies open was nibbling a sandwich. His friend was putting a pacamac in a duffle bag.

Maybe it *is* a sad little world. But the point is, it's *my* sad little world – *our* sad little world. And we shouldn't be ashamed of it. The Oval may be a giant bowl of pastel coloured bucket seats to kids like Mark, but to me it is a civilised oasis in an urban wasteland. It is a place to fritter the day away alone with my thoughts. For a cricket ground is a refuge for artists and for thinkers. After all, it's hard to imagine Aristotle standing on the football terraces, taunting the away supporters, threatening to put the sandal in after the match, or Michelangelo playing pool down the pub with his mates. No, this is where they'd be – with us, looking up Vibert Greene's vital statistics in their *Playfair* annuals. And not until you have sat alone in a cricket ground on a Thursday afternoon in July waiting for it to stop hailing so that Eddie Hemmings can resume his innings, will you ever really understand the complexity of the human condition.

And we should hold our heads up high when we play the game too. Ignore the sneering remarks and smirking faces as we squeeze into our whites which once again seem to have shrunk during the winter. Cricket infidels will never comprehend what drives us to venture out into the far-flung corners of the Home Counties to make complete fools of ourselves. And they mistake for madness the glint in our eyes of the missionary zeal we have to spread the gospel and proselytise the provinces. I have played for school, college, club and village, and I am now a cricketing gypsy offering my services to various harassed captains who find themselves 'short on a Sunday'. So I've felt the special camaraderie that only comes from standing huddled together in a changing room with ten other blokes in damp flannels waiting for it to stop raining, the heady cocktail of aromas – feet, linseed oil, and stale fishpaste sandwiches – hanging in the air.

Last but not least in this cricketing life there has been my unofficial role for a quarter of a century as a constant spiritual presence for England and Surrey sides. All over the world and at all hours of the night I have communed with England touring teams via my trannie under the bedclothes or latterly from the sofa-bed watching Sky's satellite coverage. The Rev. Wingfield-Digby might have been wafting about the England dressing room sharing a consoling psalm with Mark Ramprakash, but it was me 12,000 miles away doing my best Uri Geller thinking positive bit, willing the poor bugger to lay bat on ball.

This book is part autobiography, part examination of

an obsession that has endured for some 25 years, part confessional of the internal workings of that most confused of human beings – the thirtysomething male – and part whinge. The autobiographical elements are there because the context of the obsession helps to explain the obsession itself. The stranglehold the obsession exerts on the male psyche says more about men than a whole tanktop (or whatever the collective noun is) of sociologists will ever tell you. And a whinge because I am English and we have a crummy team that plays under a crummy system, and we all need to get things off our chests sometimes.

So, sod my little companion staring at his watch. He doesn't know what he's missing.

And another thing: to this day he still hasn't the foggiest who Jim Foat is!

CHAPTER ONE

Obsession
The one-track mind of a
cricket fanatic

M. Bussell Select XI v Celebrity XI

Date: 28 June 1973   *Venue:* Chemistry Lab   *Toss:* Celebrity XI

M.Bussell Select XI

J.Edrich	c Rubble b Welch	84
G.Boycott	b Gray	2
Asif Iqbal	b Gray	6
C.Lloyd	st Worth b Tintin	37
A.Greig	c&b Welch	41
* M.Bussell	c Holder b Glaze	0
G.Sobers	lbw b Welch	11
† A.Knott	c Feldman b Tintin	9
J.Snow	c Worth b Glaze	27
B.Bedi	b Hill	286
D.Lillee	not out	93
Total		596

Celebrity XI

N.Holder	c Lloyd b Lillee	17
S.George	c Snow b Lillee	18
V.Tracey	lbw b Bussell	53
* P.Glaze	st Knott b Bussell	0
B.Rubble	c&b Bedi	68
M.Feldman	st Knott b Snow	5
B.Hill	run out	22
† H.Worth	lbw b Bussell	28
L.Gray	c Bussell b Greig	169
Tintin	c Knott b Sobers	1
R.Welch	not out	77
Total		458

B eing an eleven-year-old boy will always be confusing and difficult. It is a time when the voice oscillates embarrassingly in a vocal range anywhere between Alan Ball and Frank Bruno, often in mid-syllable; and in a cricketing sense it is a time when a choice has to be made whether to stick with the once cosy, now rather tight, pink soapdish of a box or graduate to the roomier white box with padded rim. But somehow if you are an eleven-year-old boy who is obsessed with cricket, life is even more confusing and difficult than ever. People don't understand you. Mothers, neighbours, even your own friends furrow brows and make worried noises about you. After all, you should be doing what all other normal eleven-year-old boys are doing – building a tree-house, shooting at starlings with an air pistol, or masturbating furiously. You certainly shouldn't be sitting in a dark room on a Sunday afternoon in the middle of a heatwave scoring the televised John Player League match between Nottinghamshire and Derbyshire.

I used to, and, frankly, I was considered odd. So odd in fact that my mother tried to persuade me to take up what she considered to be the more socially acceptable pastime of trainspotting instead. At least, she figured, it would get me out of the house. I could take my thermos, books and pencil case to a windswept railway station, and get out from under her feet so she could watch Tony Curtis in *The Persuaders* rather than Mike Smedley in the Notts middle order.

As with all boyhood obsessions it was all-engulfing –

what you might call an extreme case of anoraksia nervosa. Every day, I cut out of the *Daily Telegraph* the county scoreboard and glued it into a scrapbook. Religiously, I would double check batting totals and match them against bowling analyses to see if they tallied. From time to time I would find errors which disconcerted me greatly. It was one of the first indications that the adult world was fallible and as prone to getting its sums wrong as my little brother. I took my ability to spot these errors as further proof, along with the wispy shrub of pubic hair sprouting under my 'Y'-fronts, that I was on the threshold of manhood, and considered the errata announcements in the paper a few days later as a personal apology to me. But too often for my father's liking he would open the paper to peruse the racing results, only to find a gaping hole. I had an unquenchable appetite for cricket statistics that despite his daily threats of reprisals showed no sign of abating. Either he was going to have to find another way to feed my habit, or take up *découpure* himself.

Domestic harmony was secured with his purchase of my first *Wisden Almanack*. This yellow tome of facts and figures opened up fresh vistas – not just contemporary statistics and recent history but ancient records detailing the feats of men with wonderful sounding names: F.R.Spofforth, K.S.Ranjitsinhji, P.G.H.Fender, G.O.'Gubby' Allen, The Nawab of Pataudi. They were people who if not dead had stopped playing thirty or forty years ago, but they were an important part of the folklore of my chosen world and I made it my duty to know it.

My family paid a price for this devotion. Hardly a car journey of any length could pass without me reciting titbits of cricket trivia and my poor grandmother was dragooned during the regular power cuts at the time into testing me on my knowledge – Pakistan's Test captains in order, or Indian

10

bowlers who had taken more than 100 wickets in Tests. Frail as she is now in her nineties, here is a woman who never fully mastered the implications of decimalisation but could still tell you how many times Fazal Mahmood captained Pakistan. It was as if I was swotting for my cricketing Barmitzvah and that on my thirteenth birthday I would recite before my entire family and friends the all-time top Test batting averages.

After school, with my trusty trannie pressed to my ear, I would rush back home to catch the post-tea session of the Test match on BBC2. When cricket wasn't being televised I would set myself cricketing conundrums: how many different words could I get out of VENKATARAGHAVAN? Or, could I pick an alliterative England team – Brian Bolus, John Jameson, Peter Parfitt, etc? Some nights Dad would find me late at night sitting up in bed mumbling behind a Latin text book. He would pat me on the head and shoot me a rare look of parental pride before telling me not to overdo the studying and to get some sleep. It was only when I spectacularly failed my Latin 'O' level that it became clear that those sleepless nights had been spent conjugating (as it were) international wicket-keepers rather than Latin verbs.

It was hard trying to be a cricket obsessive in the early seventies – much harder than football which a number of my friends had chosen to be the object of their juvenile fixation. We cricket fanatics didn't have soccer stars albums to occupy us. There was no swapping of Ken Higgs for Roy Virgin going on in the playground; no boy with sixteen Stuart Turners he didn't know what to do with. And there wasn't a weekly comic in the *Shoot!* vein for us to delve into. So we never knew all that important stuff, like what car Brian Luckhurst drove, or whether Barry Wood's favourite meal was steak and chips. But somehow, despite being denied the oxygen of news, gossip, and trivia on which all sports fans thrive, it just made us even more enterprising in seeking it out.

Living as we did then in the suburban sprawl of Marlow in Buckinghamshire, I was at least thirty miles away from the nearest first-class cricket ground. Uxbridge was the closest but traditionally hosted only a couple of Middlesex games in August when we were inconveniently away on holiday. Lord's and The Oval were that bit further east and Northampton further away still to the north. The sporadic Minor County fixtures that Bucks played at Marlow or High Wycombe represented a meagre diet – a thin gruel of faceless players who only warranted a few lines in *Wisden*. Deprived as I was, I had to take advantage of the merest glimmer of cricketing glamour when it came our way and so the prospect of Michael Parkinson's Showbiz XI playing an Old England XI was too much to resist. I knew these jolly japes for charity were far from the real thing, but beggars could not be choosers and so my poor family were press-ganged into going.

I recall Ernie Wise got the biggest laugh of the day when he reprised an old Morecambe and Wise sketch by going out to bat with a bat three foot wide (They don't write them like that anymore!). Michael Aspel was there, as was Bill Grundy, the presenter, with his unfeasibly gruff voice booming cries of 'wait on' to his batting partner, but the most surreal sight of the day by some way was watching Gerald Harper (he of *Hadleigh* fame) opening the batting with Jesus. Yes, Jesus. And in Maidenhead too. Well, that's how it seemed to me and my brother. Still I suppose if you were going to resurrect yourself two thousand years later the M4 corridor would be as good a place as any, what with its proximity to Heathrow airport and everything. Luckily, my father was on hand to make clear the distinctions between television fiction and reality and to point out that this was not actually Jesus but the actor, Robert Powell, who was playing at the time the eponymous hero of the epic TV serial *Jesus of Nazareth*. Just as well we cleared that up for, frankly, the day's events would not have made good biblical copy – 'And lo, Jesus did rise again and get involved in a run out with *Nationwide* anchorman Michael Barratt.'

Clearly, for the dedicated cricket follower that I was, this stay of abstinence from a recognised temple of worship could not continue for long, and after protracted badgering, my father took me to see Surrey v Gloucestershire at The Oval. There, despite an imperious 153 from Zaheer and some rumbustious batting from Mike Proctor, I fell for the more prosaic talents of John Edrich. I suppose it was love of sorts. I had snogged Janet Halpin on the back seat of the coach following a school trip to Hatfield House and Lucy Perkins had shown me her 'front bottom' in her father's garden shed, but really neither experience provided the same frisson as watching or even reading about an Edrich century. In 1974, when Edrich returned from the international wilderness to score a hundred against India at Manchester, I was overcome with joy and pride. That night I lay in bed too excited to sleep, fantasising about the eulogistic reports in the next day's papers. Nothing could match the feeling. Not even the prospect of a private viewing of a whole classroom of front bottoms.

Of course, such idolatry comes easily to twelve-year-olds. The girls in my school were all obsessed with a Bay City Roller called Woody and tied tartan scarves to their wrists as a totem of their devotion. I restricted myself to an elasticated white sweatband as worn by my cricket hero, John. I was very much alone, however, in this obsession. Unlike fans of The Osmonds or David Cassidy, nobody screamed or fainted when John appeared in public. Quite the contrary actually. I vividly remember on a rare shopping expedition with my mother being appalled that when John opened the new sports section of Bentalls, the Kingston-based department store, people openly ignored him and rooted through bargain bins of tennis socks during his speech. Others mistook him for a shop assistant and asked for directions to Bedding or Kitchenware. Did they not realise that they were in the presence of genius – a man who only eight summers ago had flailed the New Zealand attack about Headingley for 310 not out? I was devastated. I got his autograph twice just to help him save face in front of the supercilious Bentalls PR johnny. For a few hours, however, his star dimmed in my eyes, but eventually I was able to console myself that my rapport with John was of a more rarified personal sort: not the common or garden faddish obsession of a bunch of teenyboppers, but something far more profound and dignified.

But if my parents were worried that they had 'lost' me to cricket, it was their own fault. As Larkin might have put it: 'They fuck you up, your mum and dad, and then worst of all, they get you interested in cricket.' Peter West may have looked like a Moonie elder but it was some years before he had access to my mind via the airwaves. No, it was my own father who had sown the first seeds when he bought me my first cricket set. From Woolworths but made in Pakistan, an elastic band was wrapped around four stumps, a bat and a ball, and it was in the back garden that my cricket indoctrination started. Dad was from a strictly orthodox sect. His mentors were the fire-and-brimstone merchants of Tyson and Trueman, and the 'they shall not pass' exponents of batsmanship like Bailey and Washbrook. He didn't believe in mollycoddling. I had to learn the hard way. That is why my first memories of cricket with Dad are not of him dispensing gentle underarm lobs, but of him bowling leg cutters off a full run that started in the vegetable

14

patch. When not bowling, Dad would be keeping wicket in Mum's oven gloves and demolishing the stumps every other ball as he appealed to the imaginary square-leg umpire.

It was a hard school but some important lessons were learned. I learned to sell my wicket dearly, because I might get only one chance with Dad playing. You see, Dad, rather like Javed Miandad playing a Test in Pakistan, could never be out leg before wicket. He could be snared right in front, but there was always some excuse – a faint nick, missing leg stump, whatever. You had to bowl him neck and crop, and even then he had been known to claim it was a no-ball. So I learned to play hard. I never walked. I threw tantrums over decisions I didn't like, threatening to take my bat and ball away. I sledged my younger brother. I bowled beamers at my father if he batted too long. And I tampered openly with the ball. (I discovered if you soaked it in the goldfish pond before you started a spell it kept alarmingly low and made scoring difficult.) In short, I played like any Australian or Pakistani Test player.

Now, we are constantly told that English cricket is soft and the cause is variously attributed to the demotivating effect of the constant grind of county cricket, or the anti-competitive culture of comprehensive schools, or the banning of the birch, depending on what newspaper you read. Well, I have absolutely no idea why our Test players always look like shrinking violets compared to those from other countries but I do know it is not genetic. You watch any group of eleven-year-olds playing and it's dog eat dog. They're not going to give their wicket away. They'll bat until dark rather than have to field. David Lloyd is wasting his time with videos, and buzz words written on cards, and 'Rule, Britannia' blaring out in the dressing room, he should just tell the lads to play like they used to when they were eleven. There might be the occasional squabble about whose turn it is to bat, but the mean-spirited tenacity will be there by the bucket.

So what happens in the intervening years? Clearly, English cricket disproves the Jesuit notion of 'Give me the boy until he is seven years old, and I will give you the man', for by the time our cricket-loving lad from Barnsley is fifteen, he's found another way to have fun on grass, whereas the fifteen-year-old from Bangalore has more than likely made his debut for India and signed a multi-million rupee contract to advertise mopeds.

That said, it's obviously in these formative years that one's basic technique and mental approach is forged. Colin Cowdrey is supposed to have learned to bat on a tennis court in the grounds of the family home in India. In time-honoured fashion on his return from work, Cowdrey senior would have his son practising after tea and would toss cricket balls to him until sundown. The story goes that if the young Cowdrey played through the offside the ball was stopped by the tennis court net, but that all legside hits had to be retrieved by Colin himself. This soon became a laborious process, especially so under a hot Simla sun, but it was an education that was to pay dividends in later years as Cowdrey developed into a Test player with an array of offside strokes that his contemporaries could only envy.

My own batting style is, however, the product of much less exotic circumstances and not so much shaped by the last days of the Raj as the dying days of Reg. Reg Brown was our next door neighbour. A man in his early seventies, he had lost his wife Beryl three weeks before we moved in. Apparently, Mrs Brown had left the house one morning feeling right as rain only to collapse two hours later in the High Street outside The Happy Kebab. It had, according to the neighbourhood, knocked the stuffing out of him and from then on he lived a rather miserable, withdrawn, even bitter life doing what pensioners do: gardening, driving slowly on Bank Holidays, and confiscating kids' footballs. In fact a young boy soon realises that there are, broadly speaking, two types of old person – there are those that ruffle your hair and call you 'whippersnapper', who slip you mint humbugs when you visit them and sponsor you lavishly for doing a few laps of the school pool, and there are those who'll think nothing of slashing your spacehopper if you so much as touch their manicured lawn let alone try to retrieve a frisbee from their clematis. Reg Brown had his check slippers very much in the latter camp. He hated kids, but in particular, he hated kids who trampled all over his prize-winning camellias. His back garden was a veritable Bermuda Triangle for all types of ball, kite, or shuttlecock, and retrieving them required a plan of absolute precision – three of you creating a diversion by singing 'Men of Harlech' outside his front door while another vaulted over the back fence from a wooden horse, located the ball and then ran for it without looking back until you reached the safety of home or Switzerland, whichever was easiest.

Thus I learned never to hit the ball through the legside towards Reg Brown's fence and certainly never in the air. He died when I was fifteen but too late for me to undo the damage done and break old habits. If I were a believer in the afterlife, I might be able to envisage a contented Reg reunited with his beloved Beryl outside the Pearly Gates and joyfully handing back stray shuttlecocks to young cherubs enjoying a spot of celestial badminton, but I'm not. Nevertheless, Reg has achieved some small level of immortality for his legacy can be seen regularly on Sunday afternoons during the summer as I pat legside full tosses back to the bowler.

'Why cricket?' is the question I am constantly asked. Why

not an obsession with football? Or rugby? Well, I like both those sports too and a Gascoigne curler from 25 yards or a jinking Guscott run can still tickle the adrenal gland. Yet both have always been soft drugs for me, not the hard addictive drug that cricket is. The England football team failing to reach the World Cup finals is a real downer, but England getting massacred in an Ashes series is like a really bad trip followed by a period of cold turkey as I wait for the winter tour to begin. I have just about forgiven Peter Bonetti for his madness in Mexico in 1970 but Mike Denness – the coward of 1974–75? Never.

The reasons for this addiction are unclear. I suppose the rather formal elegance of crisp white flannels had a certain childhood appeal. There seemed something very sophisticated about a sport played in long trousers. There was also the allure of being in the spotlight. All kids constantly crave attention and cricket is one of the few sports that isolates the individual performance from that of the team. And there was also the thrill of cracking the secret code of the scorer's hieroglyphics, the complex language that allows anorak to communicate with anorak.

However, 'why' questions are notoriously difficult to answer, as those of you with young children will testify. Why do we have eyebrows? Why does broccoli taste disgusting? Why are bogies green? These are all questions I have struggled to answer in recent months. But of course when people ask 'Why cricket?', it is a much more complex question than it seems at first. Behind it lurks a whole set of prejudices which allied to an incredulous inflection in the voice of the questioner betray a disdain for all cricket lovers. This might sound like the advanced stages of paranoia but I can prove its veracity. Conjure up in your mind if you will the stereotypical image of the fans of our three national games. What have you got? The football fan is a working-class boy made good with a smart set of wheels, a mobile phone and a penchant for velvet-collared camel coats. The rugby lover is a hale and hearty sort of cove, possibly a tad deficient in the chin department but standing his full strapping six-foot height in his orange corduroys and Barbour jacket. Whereas the cricket fan is bespectacled, drinks real ale, reads Terry Pratchett books, and when he's not at the cricket is either building a to-scale matchstick model of the *Cutty Sark* or conducting a timorous romance on the Internet with a lab technician called Ruth who still lives with her mother. None of the three is a particularly flattering portrait, but we can all see which is the least attractive. That's the way people think of us. In fact, in their eyes, if cricket lovers were to be privatised, the regulatory body would be called OFNERD.

So, perhaps it is worth trying to change this somewhat warped perspective of us by tackling head on some of the underlying prejudices. First, cricket is not weedy. OK, so we dress up in nice white trousers and woolly jumpers and stop for lunch and tea, but it has been calculated that a batsman facing the likes of Thomson, Ambrose or Donald has just over a quarter of a second to assess the line, trajectory and likely bounce of the ball before selecting the appropriate shot. The game requires supernatural reflexes and eye-to-hand co-ordination. Otherwise, as Mike Gatting found to his cost in 1986 against Malcolm Marshall, it is only a matter of time before your nose is pebbledashed across your fizzog. My own personal catalogue of cricket injuries – a broken thumb, two broken fingers, a chipped tooth, and a cracked toe – may be a short vainglorious entry in the roll-call of cricket's victims but it goes some way to disabuse the cynical view that cricket is a weedy game.

Second, cricket is not boring. Only to the uninitiated is it boring with its short bursts of activity followed by longer periods of inactivity. But understanding this rhythm is essential to understanding cricket. A game of cricket is like a symphony. Every ball is a beat in the symphony; every over is a phrase, and the melody of the match fluctuates accordingly. A ball that takes a wicket or gets hit for four changes the tempo – the batsmen get on top for a while, the bowling side strikes back, but you have to know the sequence and context of events to appreciate their significance. That is why edited highlights on television are so unsatisfactory. If we return to our analogy, the highlights are like a symphony with all the low notes removed. It sounds similar but you know it's not how it should be. So next time a loved one tries to jemmy you off the couch so that you can escort them to Texas Homecare, tell them to mend their philistine ways and savour with you the sporting equivalent of Mahler. Then, having bathed your black eye, rush out and buy that trellis and the new window boxes and try to make it back before close of play.

Finally, cricket is not predictable as its detractors would have it. It may be possible to discern a pattern: the three-hour drive in the contraflow of the M11 every Sunday, a clean bowled duck, not getting a bowl, and dropping a dolly catch, but it is just as possible that next time it will be a century (OK, a fluent 30 anyway), three wickets for 20, and a diving catch off your own bowling. For what is a century if it is not a duck that was allowed this time to blossom and bear fruit? A faint nick on the ball rather than a miss by a fraction of an inch is all that separates glorious success from ignominious failure. The whole enterprise is subject to the whim of Lady Luck; and every ball provides scope for her capriciousness. That is why every ball is loaded with expectation. There are no dull moments; just brief periods of respite in the mounting tension.

Once you have grasped what cricket is about, squeezing

into shorts, and throwing yourself about in the mud, trying to get a sheep's bladder down the other end of a field somehow seems a bit daft. I don't suppose for one minute that I could see at eleven years old what I can see now, but some of the joyous mysteries of cricket must have rubbed off. Certainly, its glorious contradictions were clear to me even as a spotty youth in 1973. Here was a game that was stately, yet fiercely aggressive. It could be long drawn out, but equally it could be grippingly climactic. It was a team game that relied wholly on individual performance. It was comic (Fred Swarbrook) and tragic (Keith Fletcher), graceful (Barry Richards) and ugly (Basharat Hassan).

Once you have been bitten by the cricket bug, life is spent constantly improvising contests of bat and ball. When I left university I moved to London to take up employment with an advertising agency. There I was to share an office with Charles, a rather tubby account executive whose principal achievement hitherto had been the successful re-launch of the Bounty Bar. This, as far as I could work out, had centred on few innovations save the removal of that cardboard shelf inside the wrapper on which the two chocolate bars used to sit. Notwithstanding my fear that all over the country there were unsupported Bounty Bars and that a confectionery disaster on the scale of Aberfan was just around the corner, I was prepared to accept that I was in the company of a visionary. When Charles devised 'office cricket', a trial of stamina and technique which involved fending away a golf ball with an umbrella, I knew I was.

Matches lasted days as we fitted play around the inconvenience of work. The batsman was required to defend his wicket (the hatstand) on a parquet floor that allowed alarming Caribbean-style bounce. Close fielders in the form of waste paper bins and filing cabinet drawers surrounded the batsman; one run was scored when contact was made, two if you got it under either desk, four if you got it through the narrow gap between the pot plant and the door that led to the office of our secretary, who acted as umpire in the event of any dispute, and six if you hit the Sasco Year Planner on the wall. The devilish 'throat ball' was used increasingly as an innings progressed and rapped knuckles were commonplace. I guarantee Alec Stewart wouldn't have lasted ten minutes with his dodgy digits. Keenly fought battles were halted only after the office window was smashed for the second time. The first breakage was explained away as the result of a pigeon flying into our rather large Regency sash but it was difficult to ascribe the same explanation to an identical hole two weeks later. Our boss was never going to accept an epidemic of low-flying kamikaze pigeons, so we drew stumps once and for all. If you think Dickie Bird's final Test was emotional, you should have been with us the day we put the golf ball in the drawer and hung up our umbrella.

Luckily for me, I was engaged in a similar contest with my flatmate, Dave. Making full use of a long corridor in the flat a foam ball was bowled at a batsman armed with a cardboard poster tube. Fast bowlers were allowed to bowl overarm emerging at full pelt from the bathroom. Spinners had to bowl underarm but could extract prodigious turn with floated deliveries outside the off stump that hit the join of the carpet and the kitchen lino. Ever since the Indian tour of 1971 I had fallen in love with the guile and trickery of Messrs Bedi, Chandrasekhar, Venkat and co. who put batsmen through a slow torture of gentle, looping spinners. Not for me the belligerence and brawn of fast bowlers, it was these twirlymen that I aspired to, these exponents of the subtler arts of bowling with their flight, loop and spin. I worked hard at bowling an offside line and hitting that carpet join and many a time Dave was gated aiming an airy drive in the direction of the fridge. It was Dave's considerable misfortune to be sharing a flat with me. Had he shared with John Emburey, he would doubtless have been far more successful with John spearing the ball leg stump to a packed legside field in the sitting room, economical but wicketless.

However, even these approximations to cricket require a good deal of space and someone else to play with and, as every eleven-year-old knows only too well, sometimes there's no alternative than to do it on your own. Hence the invention of pocket cricket, otherwise known as Owzat. This game operated solely in the imagination and called for the rolling of two small hexagonal barrels, although a subtly marked pencil often proved more discreet for use in certain situations such as the classroom. At my school, there were, as far as I could divine, only three good things about chemistry: (i) you could usually set fire to Mark Cocker's blazer with a bunsen burner, (ii) you could usually lock Mark Cocker in the fume cupboard. (For your information Cocker had grown up in Yorkshire and moved down south and into our school when he was twelve. He had the sense of self-irony of Geoff Boycott and the open-mindedness of Ray Illingworth, but unfortunately for him none of the courage of Brian Close and there was no way thirty 'southern softies', as he endearingly called us, were going to let him get away with it. His was a life in hell and I often wonder what Cocker is doing now, some twenty years later – probably wreaking his revenge on humanity, making the public pay for his traumatic experiences at school – a dentist perhaps, or a bailiff, or a television sit-com writer.) But the best thing about chemistry was: (iii) you could play Owzat with relative impunity while others were doing tedious experiments in petrie dishes.

The scorecard listed at the top of this chapter was found in the back of an old school exercise book of mine that for some twenty years had gathered dust in a box in my parents' loft. This box was a veritable treasure trove of seventies memorabilia. Among the detritus of my childhood were my Esso Mexico 70 World Cup coin collection minus Paul Madeley and Brian Labone; a *Tiger* comic supplement with all the Montreal Olympic results; one of those huge biros that allowed you to write in fifteen different colours and whose design owed more to Ann Summers than to Bic; various soccer stars albums; a Rolf Harris stylophone; and a host of old school books chock-full of recorded Owzat matches. Perhaps more than anything else in that box it is these entries in scratchy handwriting that gives the most profound insight into the workings of the adolescent mind. The Hard-on XI captained by Mary Millington lost to a Top of the Pops XI despite Julie Christie's 174 not out and a wayward spell of bowling from Suzi Quatro, while an entry in the match between The Artists and The TV Detectives reads:

'V. Van Gogh . . . run out . . . 6 (Didn't hear the call)'

A lot of these matches were played solo and late at night as I waited for my parents to go to bed so that I could turn on the old black and white telly in my bedroom and watch the continental movie on ITV. Reading today's newspapers one could be mistaken for thinking that Euroscepticism is a recent phenomenon but back in the seventies we were just as exercised by all things foreign. The adjective 'continental' often suggested something depraved. I remember a great aunt of mine commenting censoriously on society's embrace of the continental quilt, which she clearly saw as the bedlinen of Sodom and Gomorrah, declaring that she would 'never sleep under anything continental'. And her views about the continental breakfast were just as trenchant. For her, there was something degenerate about a breakfast that could be readily consumed in bed, but this debased culture of the continent sounded right up this eleven-year-old boy's street and my appointment with the continental movie became a regular one. These films invariably involved a travelling salesman with large sideburns romping around with a comely young blonde woman who had an irritating habit of covering the best bits of her shapely body with a bath towel every time she moved. Occasionally, however, her bath towel technique would let her down and we'd all get a glimpse of prime German buttock which was enough to keep you interested. But during the ad breaks and the boring sequences between bed scenes, Owzat was the best way to stave off sleep.

Other matches were played in class. Fred Bristow was my partner in crime and the best environment was found in the relative freedom of chemistry lessons. So while 'Doc' Orchard, our chemistry master, droned on about the special properties of hydrochloric acid – all we knew was that it made Cocker yelp when poured on to his hand – Fred and I picked our teams and play commenced.

Perhaps the most remarkable feature of the two teams chosen is that even some twenty years on, the Select XI would probably not change much. Lara would replace Asif and the post-Packer-disgraced Greig would make way for Ian Botham but my cricketing heroes have remained fairly constant. Quite the opposite, however, can be said for the Celebrity XI. How today could I not find room for Woody Allen, Joe Orton, Nelson Mandela, Alan Bennett and Jennifer Aniston? I mean what was I thinking of?! Peter Glaze as captain?! Harry Worth as wicket-keeper?! No, only Slade lead singer Noddy Holder, currently experiencing a renaissance would be retained, and then only for a certain kitsch appeal. Out goes pouting Susan George (*Straw Dogs* being but a distant memory) and in comes our Jennifer from *Friends*. Virgil Tracey, despite his 50, would have to go back to Tracey Island and resume his piloting of Thunderbird 2 and conveniently, skipper Glaze, whose trademark 'doh' on *Crackerjack* won him the affection of the nation's youth in the early seventies, could be replaced by Homer Simpson, today's man with the comedy 'doh'. Benny Hill and Harry Worth would make way for the more sophisticated comedy practitioners of Woody Allen and Alan Bennett, and Les Gray of Mud (remember 'Tiger Feet'?) can hot-foot it despite his big hundred. As for Tintin, well I am now led to believe that his creator Hergé was a fascist, while Raquel Welch is related (albeit by marriage) to Fred Trueman. So, enough said there.

What this shows quite clearly is how the sporting side of the brain is retarded. As we age so our social and cultural perspective changes. We experience new and varied things and see the heroes of yesterday in a broader context. Their limitations become more apparent. In 1972, Benny Hill's 'Ernie (The Fastest Milkman in the West)' was the funniest thing I'd ever heard. Now, we've got BoyZone who are in their own completely different way much funnier. But when it comes to the cricketers, I find it much harder to shed those early loyalties. Has there ever been a better wicket-keeper/batsman than Alan Knott? Or a better all-rounder than Sobers? Have we witnessed a more destructive batsman than Clive Lloyd? Or a more resilient one than Boycott? Somehow their feats on the field seem more heroic and irrevocably etched on the memory than the achievements of the current players. Atherton's vigil in Johannesburg and Cork's hat-trick were wondrous moments in recent years but their failings in the here-and-now are all too visible. It will take the passage of time to filter out the horrid noughts and the hapless overs of long hops.

Of the players of my youth, however, I remain in constant awe for we all view the sporting world through the impressionable eyes of an eleven-year-old. Even my father, who is now in his mid-sixties, is locked in the time warp of the eleven-year-old. He'll swear blind that England has never had a better batsman than Wally Hammond, and if you try to tell him that Frank Tyson would today be considered barely medium paced, he'll pour his pint over your head. For him, today's players are but mutant forms of the gods he remembers from his schooldays. And it helps to explain (though heaven knows why we should be so magnanimous) why Messrs Bailey and Trueman constantly think that if they were teamed with any two of Brian Statham, Les Jackson or Derek Shackleton, they would knock over every current Test team for under a hundred.

This retarded state of mind also makes it clear that, though I like to feel I can be rational in my thinking and responsible in my actions about most things in life, when it comes to cricket I froth at the mouth every time Craig White is picked for England, and watch whole overs from Waqar and Wasim at the England tail from behind the sofa. Cricket proves, if it ever needed to be done, that I am but a child in a skin that's too big for me (and getting bigger all the time).

Cricket has also played with the concept of time in another fundamental sense. The standard units of time – minutes, hours, days, weeks, months, etc. – are supplemented by the more arbitrary timetable of the cricket fixture list and as an aid to memory is much more effective. I can remember quite clearly the day I discovered I had passed the 12-plus because Bev Congdon was scoring a huge hundred against England at Lord's. The day my girlfriend told me that she was pregnant with what turned out to be our twin daughters was the day England were staring down the barrel of defeat against the West Indies in Jamaica and Atherton had just received one of the most ferocious maulings from a fast bowler since that twilight torture Close and Edrich went through at Old Trafford in 1976.

Try it yourself. Pick a landmark in your lifetime and see if a Test match or village game doesn't come flooding back. Can you remember, for instance, the day you lost your virginity? Sure, you recall most of the salient details – you were seventeen years old, her name was Vicky and you did it in the back of her mother's Hillman Imp . . . whatever. But can you name the date? I couldn't, but then I did remember that on the same day Alan Butcher made his debut against India at The Oval in 1979, a party that evening at a friend's house featured a frantic and sweaty encounter with a girl called Carol up against the chest freezer in the utility room. Alan and Carol are obviously blissfully unaware of the synchronised relevance of these two events, but they are inextricably linked in my mind. I can't now think of one without thinking of the other. Butcher was caught off the bowling of Venkat for 14 that day and his hopeless, awkward prodding and poking mirrored my own debut that night. Fortunately for me, while Alan Butcher never got to play for England again, I was given another chance some months later and after much reflection about my technique during the close season.

This is why flicking through *Wisden* or an old scorebook is much more than just a refamiliarisation with historical cricket statistics. It is a diary or photo album triggering all sorts of associated memories and were it not for cricket goodness knows how I would have been able to work out that I first got my end away on 30 August 1979 – an insignificant date in the rich tapestry of history, but for Alan Butcher and myself a date to remember.

I wouldn't go so far as to say that cricket gives a meaning

to life but it does offer a framework – something to cling on to in the eddy of existence as the flotsam and jetsam of your love life, career and family swirl around you. It is our great fortune that we have chosen cricket (or cricket chose us) as the object of our obsession. But it is our great misfortune that it should be English cricket.

CHAPTER TWO

Does He Take Sugar?
The psychosis of being an
England supporter

England v West Indies (3rd Test)

Date: 23–7 August 1973   *Venue:* Lord's   *Toss:* West Indies

West Indies

R.C.Fredericks	c Underwood b Willis	51
†D.L.Murray	b Willis	4
*R.B.Kanhai	c Greig b Willis	157
C.H.Lloyd	c and b Willis	63
A.I.Kallicharran	c Arnold b Illingworth	14
G.St A.Sobers	not out	150
M.L.C. Foster	c Willis b Greig	9
B.D.Julien	c and b Greig	121
K.D.Boyce	c Amiss b Greig	36
V.A.Holder	not out	23
L.R.Gibbs	did not bat	
Extras	(B1, LB14, W1, NB8)	24
Total	(8 wickets declared)	652

Bowling	O	M	R	W
Arnold	35	6	111	0
Willis	35	3	118	4
Greig	33	2	180	3
Underwood	34	6	105	0
Illingworth	31.4	3	114	1

ENGLAND

G.Boycott	c Kanhai b Holder	4	c Kallicharran b Boyce	15
D.L.Amiss	c Sobers b Holder	35	c Sobers b Boyce	10
B.W.Luckhurst	c Murray b Boyce	1	(4)c Sobers b Julien	12
F.C.Hayes	c Fredericks b Holder	8	(5)c Holder b Boyce	0
K.W.R.Fletcher	c Sobers b Gibbs	68	(6) not out	86
A.W.Greig	c Sobers b Boyce	44	(7)lbw b Julien	13
R.Illingworth	c Sobers b Gibbs	0	(8)c Kanhai b Gibbs	13
†A.P.E.Knott	c Murray b Boyce	21	(3)c Murray b Boyce	5
G.G.Arnold	c Murray b Boyce	5	c Fredericks b Gibbs	1
R.G.D.Willis	not out	5	c Fredericks b Julien	0
D.L.Underwood	c Gibbs b Holder	12	b Gibbs	14
Extras	(B6, LB4, W3, NB17)	30	(B9, W1, NB14)	24
Total		233		193

Bowling	O	M	R	W	O	M	R	W
Holder	15	3	56	4	14	4	18	0
Boyce	20	7	50	4	16	5	49	4
Julien	11	4	26	0	18	2	69	3
Gibbs	18	3	39	2	13.3	3	26	3
Sobers	8	0	30	0	4	1	7	0
Foster	1	0	2	0				

It can surely be no coincidence that Lord's should have virtually the same name as that other famous shrine. The difference is that pilgrims who go to the one in France on the whole leave fairly satisfied, their faith fully restored, their spiritual being reinvigorated, and their bunions miraculously cured. Whereas those of us that make the annual pilgrimage to the one in NW8 invariably leave penniless, hassled and emotionally desolate. Penniless because the seat prices charged by the TCCB are such that only the chief executives of the newly privatised utilities can afford them without remortgaging the house. Hassled because even though your MCC member friend assured you that you could collect the tickets from the office at the Grace Gates, you still have to go five rounds with one of the bowler-hatted Nazis who form the Praetorian Guard at Lord's, before they would even let you join the queue. (These guys delight in obstruction, playing life by the rule book and sniffing out a socialist from 50 yards.) Finally, emotionally desolate because after all the expense and trouble you have gone to (buying all those M&S sandwiches and smuggling in excess tins of lager in your underpants) you watched England lose eight wickets for 12 runs to a rampant Roger Binny or Dion Nash. Then there's the despair caused by the rain or Dickie and his lightmeter, the endless queuing for a beer, a programme, a seat cushion, or a pee, and worst of all, the MCC members themselves whose braying voices can be heard throughout the day advocating castration for persistent parking offenders. It is a miserable, painful experience and, yet, one that I have undertaken every year for nearly 25 years.

And God how I have suffered: hanging around in the rain during the Centenary Test of 1980 with only the manhandling of the umpires by the members to keep us entertained, watching Mudassar Nazar rip through England's top order with six for 32 in 1982, and Chetan Sharma doing the same in 1986, and Bruce French's excruciating 42 on a rain-affected Saturday in 1987, and Geoff Lawson's 74 and ninth-wicket partnership of 130 with Steve Waugh in 1989, and Trevor Franklin's barnacle impression with 101 in 1990, and Mike Gatting leaving Atherton stranded on his backside for 99 in 1993, and the 99 all out against South Africa in 1994, or the final afternoon in 1996 when England collapsed to Mushtaq Ahmed in the time it takes to roll a fag.

Masochism takes many varied forms – I understand gouging the flesh with a razor blade and burning your privates with hot needles are techniques particularly favoured by those predisposed to a spot of self-mutilation. But watching England is, I would hazard, a far subtler and ultimately more effective means of achieving the same end. Apparently, the real thrill to be had from masochism is in the anticipation prior to the application of pain. Well, in cricket we can, as happened in Bulawayo in 1996, go to the final ball of the fifth day before the exhilarating insertion of the blade. That's five whole days of anticipation before the pain. And I predict it is only a matter of time before one of us is found dead on the kitchen table wearing ladies' stockings, electric flex round the neck, and a cream cake in the mouth, with *Test Match Special* on the radio beside us.

It all started for me in 1973 on the Saturday of the third Test against the West Indies in a match that saw one of

England's largest-ever defeats. The West Indies batted first and scored over 650 with Kanhai, Sobers, and Bernard Julien (!) all making hundreds. The seventh wicket put on 231 and, for what *Wisden* states as only the second time in history, five bowlers conceded over 100 runs in the same innings. England then collapsed to 29 for three before mustering 233 in the first innings and then with the follow-on enforced collapsing again to 87 for six. A recovery of sorts ensued until midway through the fourth afternoon and England finally lost by an innings and 226 runs. It proved to be Ray Illingworth's last Test and ushered in his twenty years of isolation from the England scene until his ill-fated return as chairman of selectors in 1994. I was eleven years old and had just witnessed what was to become a recurring theme in my cricketing life – the enduring ineptitude of the England team.

Many things stick in the mind from that first trip to Lord's. In the early seventies a trip to London from the provinces was, much more so than today, like visiting a foreign country. The sheer scale and energy of the place. The bustle, the noise, traffic jams as far as the eye could see, black taxis scuttling about like beetles at feeding time, the magnificence of the buildings in central London contrasting starkly with the squalor by the Westway. And there were the people of this foreign land – dark faces and coloured robes up the Edgware Road, ringlets and yarmulkas around St John's Wood, and then at the ground, pink faces under Panama hats, and exuberant black ones in brightly coloured clothes laughing, dancing, ringing bells, slapping backs, and blowing conch shells. For those were the days when real supporters went to Test matches rather than those from the Information Technology Dept. of Barclays Bank on a corporate jolly.

The whole atmosphere was completely different to that

generated by the sparse gathering at The Oval for that
Surrey match against Gloucestershire earlier in the year.
Here, in the shadow of the majestic pavilion a carnival was
taking place as England's batsmen struggled against a gifted
West Indies attack. Boyce was all menace. Julien slithered
to the crease, a cobra in flannels, spitting in-ducking
deliveries from over the wicket. Gibbs rattled through
his probing overs off a two-yard run-up as if emerging
suddenly from a revolving door. And Sobers bowled his
medium-paced swingers, purring to the wicket like a
chauffeur-driven limousine. Every ball was bowled to the
rhythmic percussion of tin cans. Black faces shrieked their
joy. White faces muttered into their cravats. London was
most definitely a foreign country – it felt like England were
playing away. Alien forces were outside the ground too.
The afternoon session was disrupted by a bomb scare that
required the evacuation of the ground: the IRA, Dad told
me, were bombing London. It all seemed a far cry from
life at home where the theft of a garden gnome made
headline news.

The West Indians revelled in our sporting failure, the
Irish wanted our political submission and all around me
the Panama hats grumbled: 'Bloody Illingworth, just when
we needed a captain's innings!' 'Greig?! He's not English.
He's one of Bokkie's lot.' With England following on in the
evening session, Boycott, who was at that time considered
a compulsive hooker, went for a Boyce bouncer and was
caught on the boundary by Kallicharran right in front of
the Mound Stand where we were sitting. England's premier
batsman and the one most likely to relish the challenge of
a rearguard action had gone. By now the Panama hats,
stuffed to the gills with coronation chicken and half a
case of Burgundy, went puce with anger: 'Bloody Boycott!
Bloody Yorkshireman!' It seemed an odd way to choose

to spend your weekend working your way towards a full seizure. But soon I would realise that is what watching England is all about. It is my vocation to witness the misery of mediocrity and the despair of decline. In fact, it would appear to be my birthright.

Failure was not confined to home either. I was too young to appreciate the achievements of Illingworth's England side in winning the Ashes on the 1970–71 tour. My first memories of England touring are from 1972–73 when A.R.Lewis captained England in India and where having won the first Test in Delhi, they lost 2–1 over the series. India was the tour that England's better players traditionally missed in order to recharge the batteries. And it was a mixture of hubris and the strength in depth of the English professional game in the fifties and sixties that England could afford to send makeshift teams and still win. But in 1972–73, shorn of the skills and experience of Boycott, Edrich, Illingworth and Snow, who had been the core of that Ashes-winning side, England came unstuck. Since then success overseas has been an event comparable in its rarity to the appearance of Halley's Comet or Jack Bannister saying anything interesting.

Indeed, supporting England should be declared by the medical authorities as a mental illness and then two million of us, all new care in the community patients, could legitimately go on to the register. At the moment, there's no hope for us and not much in the way of help. There we sit in front of the telly, our mouths hanging open and dribbling beer, dumbstruck by events on the screen. We can't talk. We can't hear. We are cocooned from the real world. Our families worry about us behind our backs, but we just sit there waiting for Meals on Wheels (the pizza man on his moped) to arrive. OK, we're a bit better now. At least the screaming fits have stopped. But our families live in constant fear that the dark days of 1993 will return. For the 1972–73 tour of India may have been the start of the decline but unquestionably we hit rock bottom in India in 1993.

If ever you have doubted this, it is worth reminding you of the sorry tale of events. Business started in earnest on what was a short three-Test series in Calcutta and you feared the worst when you saw the make-up of the two teams selected. England chose to go in with four seamers and Salisbury, plus Hick to fill in as required. Neither Tufnell nor Emburey was risked. India, on the other hand, picked three spinners in Kumble, Chauhan and Raju, who collectively bowled 205 of the 237 overs India bowled in both innings. Hick, our part-time spinner, comfortably finished with the best match figures of five for 21 off 19 overs, but India scored 371 courtesy of a big hundred from Azharuddin and bowled us out for 163 and 286. Gooch's perennial lack of faith in spin bowling and Fletcher's chronic misreading of the pitch and conditions meant that England went into the match with an attack with about as much cutting edge as a whoopee cushion.

Fletcher had just been appointed as England coach on a lucrative five-year contract and India was to be his first tour in charge. He instantly took himself off to South Africa on a fact-finding mission to study the touring Indian players and one of his first public utterances was to write off Anil Kumble as a bowler who didn't turn it. Twenty-one wickets at 19.80 each in the series suggested that Fletch might not be the best reader of the game and his explanation that England had selected four quickies because Indian batsmen liked playing spin bowling betrayed him as a muddled thinker. It was said of Fletcher the player that (to use common cricket parlance) 'he didn't know where his off-stump was'. As a coach, we were soon to find out, he also struggled with the precise locations of his arse and his elbow. However, chairman of selectors Ted Dexter had divined a more compelling reason for England's feeble showing in Calcutta – smog. Apparently, a lot of our chaps were getting a bit chesty and it was all down to this wretched smog. He announced his intention of auditing levels of smog in other Indian cities – the Coopers and Lybrand smog ratings no doubt – and got a sharp rap over the knuckles from the Indian government for his pains. Meanwhile, back at home, doctors were called out and we were given sedatives to contain the fits.

On to Madras for the second Test where Sidhu and Tendulkar scored ebullient centuries and India amassed 560 for six declared at 3.5 runs an over. England countered with a mere 286 on what was clearly a good batting pitch and then after being forced to follow on collapsed to 99 for six before a spirited but ultimately meaningless century from Chris Lewis introduced some respectability to proceedings. England's frontline spinners, low on confidence following their omission in the first Test, took two for 274 in 70 overs between them, whereas India's spinners took 17 of the 19 wickets to fall to bowlers. Poor management of bowling resources and plain poor bowling would have been the obvious reasons for defeat, but not for the music hall act of the ventriloquist, Lord Ted, and his dummy, The Gnome. Dodgy prawns in the hotel restaurant which had inconvenienced Gooch, Gatting and Smith were to blame. Oh, and a rather smelly canal near the ground. We might have been at the bottom of the pile when it came to playing cricket, but we sure as hell led the world in excuses. At home, dosages were increased and we were given boosters for Test match days but there was dark muttering from older members of the family who recalled how Great Uncle

Jake went like this during the summer of 1948 and took years to recover.

Following defeat in Bombay (again by an innings) with Kambli hitting 224 in front of his home crowd, Dexter was at last able to put his finger on the causes of England's abject failure. A scruffy appearance – too often the Essex men had allowed their charges to traipse about in their Tetley-sponsored shellsuits – and an excess of stubble were the two points at the top of the agenda following the TCCB's post-mortem. 'We have to look at the whole matter of facial hair,' he announced. Coincidentally, the rest of us at home were under doctor's orders not to go near a razor as well. Or sharp knives. Or lawn mowers. Even a potato masher was thought too risky.

By the following summer, Dexter's excuses had taken on a new twist. England lost the second Test at Lord's to Australia by an innings and 62 runs to go 2–0 down after two matches against what was effectively a ten-man team when McDermott dropped out with an illness (twisted bowel) during the first day. It left Australia with just the three-man attack of Hughes, Warne and May, but it still proved plenty enough in a match where Australia's top five batsmen made scores of 111, 152, 164 not out, 99 and 77. This was surely the nadir of English cricket. And we could all see the problem – our bowlers were crap. But not according to Dexter. England's problems were now down to malign cosmic forces. 'We may be in the wrong sign or something,' Dexter opined, '. . . Venus may be in the wrong juxtaposition to somewhere else.' Thus carried kicking and screaming from the house, this Test marked the first hospital stay for many of us.

Every day I expected to hear news that anthropologists had made a new discovery in the evolution of man. A successor to Selsdon Man, Ted Dexter was the living embodiment of 'Upney Man' (note: for those of you unfamiliar with the London Underground map, and the District Line in particular, Upney is the next point beyond Barking). Had he applied his own Coopers and Lybrand ratings to selectors, it is doubtful whether he would have registered a reading at all and after the 3–1 defeat in the Caribbean in 1994 Dexter fell on his sword and the straight-talking, no-nonsense Illingworth took the reins.

For a while many of us showed signs of recovery. We started to discuss the future again and our families really did think we had turned the corner. They cancelled the subscription to *Lobotomy Monthly* and began talking of that holiday in Torquay they had promised us when we got better. We all hoped that this would be the end of the gibberish, but immediately Illingworth was propounding fresh scapegoats for England's travails. First, it was the unnecessary dressing-room presence of the team's chaplain, the Rev. Andrew Wingfield-Digby. Illy clearly felt that any divine guidance would come from him and not via some puffed-up parson. We were left to ponder on the style and content of Illingworth's first dressing-room sermon: 'On the first day, God created Raymond, blah, blah, blah, blah, blah, and on t'seventh he created Sunday bloody League. Now get out there and beat the boogers.'

With Wingfield-Digby back in his parish trying to gee up the local pub darts team, Illy turned his wrath on mobile phones in the dressing room and cited commercial distractions as a cause for sloppy play. When Keith Fletcher went, he assumed total command. A drawn series against a poor West Indies side presented us with something of a false dawn, but when we lost to South Africa in Cape Town at the beginning of 1996, the excuses started again. The arrival of the players' families for the New Year had apparently distracted the players and disrupted team spirit, but that doesn't explain the loss against Pakistan at home or indeed the failure to win one of the five international matches against Zimbabwe on the 1996–97 tour. As one wag in Harare put it: 'England should have left the players at home and sent out the wives in their place.'

It all reminds me of that scene in *Fawlty Towers* where Sybil is listing her mother's phobias: '. . . vans, rats, doorknobs, birds, heights, open spaces, confined spaces, etc. etc.' It paints the perfect picture of a madwoman. List the England cricket team's apparent phobias (smog, canals, prawns, stubble, planetary movements, priests, mobile phones, wives) and I am afraid much the same conclusions have to be drawn about the personnel in charge of English cricket.

Four farcical years of selectorial muddle and hokum without one of our senior cricketing officials being able to comprehend that the problems of the England cricket team lie in the structure of English cricket. With rare exception the English system breeds joyless, unimaginative cricketers who play joyless, unimaginative cricket. At times they are able to raise the levels of their performance and excel – Stewart's brace of hundreds in Barbados, Cork's debut series, Thorpe's batting against South Africa in 1994 – but so crushed are they by the burdens of meaningless cricket played before empty stands, that they have neither the physical nor mental fortitude to match the sheer brio and positive cricket of most other teams. As for us, the wretched supporters, we have been promised the full frontal lobotomy on the NHS or our own personal video tapes of Alan Mullally bowling, which while being more painful, is apparently just as effective. After that, they won't be able to hurt us anymore.

Without the radical restructuring of the game that is required, England's selectors are forced to tinker with the team drafting in new and previously discarded faces on a match-by-match basis in the hope that things will suddenly click on the day. But how much longer can they treat the national team like a dodgy set of fairy lights? A fiddle here, a fiddle there. Take one out, put another one in. When all the time the whole bloody tree is listing and about to come crashing down.

Why, too, do the selectors always fall for the same type of player when it's as plain as the nose on Ken Rutherford's face that it doesn't work? They are constantly seduced by the 'faux all-rounder' – Pringle D.R., Lewis C.C., White C., Irani R., Ealham M.A. spring readily to mind. These are the sort of players who neither bat nor bowl to Test match standard. They are bits-and-pieces players, worth their place possibly in a one-day side but never likely to take five wickets in an innings or score a hundred, which have to be the yardsticks for Test cricket. Alternatively, the selectors pick the containing spinner who gets useful lower-order runs – Miller G., Emburey J.E., Illingworth R.K. A terrific policy if scores of 12 and 23 and match figures of two for 96 ever won you a Test match but useless otherwise. These are the sort of players that make you wake up screaming, or kick the cat when you see the team announced on Ceefax. In fact if these players continue to get picked we could see an interesting development in feline evolution. On alternate Sundays during the summer cats all over the country will go into hibernation for 24 hours hiding under beds or in airing cupboards for fear of receiving their master's moccasin up their rear end.

Pringle and Lewis have long been the whipping boys for English fans, and not without good reason, but my own particular favourite from the 'faux all-rounder' category, and the heir apparent to these two, is Craig White. Now nobody likes a witchhunt and I am sure that the lad is a personable cove who tries his best, but the simple truth is I can't stick him. It could be his slingy schoolboy bowling action, or his exaggerated forward defensive poke, or even his Midge Ure-style sideburns or perhaps it's just the desperate injustice that our Australians are always worse than theirs. His scores in a short Test career so far have been: 19, 51, 9, 42, 10, 0, 23, 1, 1, 1 and 0, added to which he has a grand total of 12 wickets at over 40. Young White is a typical member of 'The Julia Somerville Club', so named because one can only assume he has in his possession photographs depicting Ray Illingworth in a compromising position with a Spanish donkey.

But the other thing greatly to his advantage, at least under Illingworth's aegis, has been his Yorkshire roots. Rhodes S.J., Illingworth R.K., Gough D., Vaughan M.P., McGrath A., Stemp R.D., Silverwood C.E.W. have all made it on to A team or full tours during Illy's reign. All cricket fans have over the years heard tales of cricket-mad Yorkshiremen bundling their heavily pregnant wives into cars and driving them hundreds of miles so that they can give birth in God's own county and thus qualify for Yorkshire. Mum's waters may have broken in Swindon but there's no way Dad's not going to make it to Sheffield. But it has come to a pretty pass when cricket-mad fathers from all parts of the country feel obliged to drive their pregnant wives to Yorkshire just so that any son and heir will be qualified to play for England, let alone the county.

Finally, in this brief trawl through the selectorial madnesses of English cricket we have those players that fit into what we might dub the 'Scuba Club'. This includes all those players so obviously out of their depth that even equipped with snorkel and flippers they would still sink without trace. Was there anyone, for instance, not a permanent resident of Broadmoor who really thought that

Radford N.V. was the answer, or that Stephenson J.P. or Brown S.J.E. would cut the Test match mustard, or that Terry V.P. (God help us!) was the missing piece in the jigsaw?

Now, I was interested to learn recently that doctors have discovered that smiling is not just a reflex social response, but that it is also good for us. They reckon a smile releases healthy endorphins throughout the system which soothe the tortured spleen and consequently increase the prospect of a lengthy life. So, on this basis, not only have these players caused us untold emotional torment, but they have also foreshortened our lives by months. We'll all know who to blame when we're having our pacemakers fitted. Tim bloody Curtis – that's who.

But if there is one player who epitomises the miserable march of English cricket over the last two decades it is, for me, Mike Gatting. It is worth perhaps reminding ourselves of the milestones in a career that started in Karachi in 1978 and ended in Perth in 1995. In the early days he reflected the ingrained inhibitions of English batting by padding up indiscriminately and getting dismissed LBW. It became such that a day at the cricket was not complete without Mike showing that anything his footballing brother, Steve, could do, he could do better. Gatting was one of the largest fairy lights in the selectors' box and they kept trying to get him to work. So, it was with some relief for them that finally in his 54th Test innings he lit up the Wankhede Stadium in Bombay with a defiant hundred, but one that ultimately proved in vain as England lost by eight wickets.

When the cavalier Gower relinquished the captaincy for the first time in 1986 following the ritual 'blackwash' in the Caribbean, the roundhead Gatting stepped into the breach. He immediately lost the two home series of 1986 but then, in what proved to be England's final success in a Test series against anyone other than New Zealand (home and away) and India (home twice), Gatting led England to victory in Australia and retained the Ashes. He returned a hero but such status was short-lived. With England looking to be cruising to victory in the 1987 World Cup, Gatting reverse swept Allan Border's fourth ball and dollied a simple catch to the wicket-keeper. The pressure then got to the lower-order batting and with Steve Waugh bowling his full repertoire of crafty slower balls, England fell agonisingly short and lost the second of their three World Cup finals. Gatting and England had seemingly conquered years of vertigo in climbing to within sight of the mountain's summit only to slip on the final stretch and fall flat on their arses. Since then we can't even round up a sherpa to show us where base camp is.

However, just prior to the World Cup, on the short tour of Pakistan. Gatting had been at the centre of a political storm following an extended and animated altercation with umpire Shakoor Rana. It was an incident that subsequently required the intervention of the Foreign Office in a way that only the sport of cricket does. Both parties displayed a stubborn petulance not becoming of grown men, with Shakoor Rana 'taking his ball away' and not allowing play to recommence, and Gatting refusing to crayon a letter of apology. It sullied relations with Pakistan for years to come and provided the backdrop for the ball-tampering scandals of the 1990s. Most irritating of all, it denied England the likelihood of victory in that Test which would have been England's first in Pakistan since 1961.

It was around the mid-eighties, too, that the vultures of the tabloid press began to take much more interest in the rotting carcass that was English cricket, chewing on juicy bits of scandal both real and fictitious. It was Botham that kick-started the feeding frenzy. So when Gatting was found having a drink with a barmaid in his Nottingham hotel room, he was unceremoniously stripped of the captaincy. The public-school upbringing of the English cricket establishment headed by P.B.H.May (Charterhouse and Cambridge) came immediately to the fore and it took a dim view of such shenanigans. As far as they were concerned Gatting knew the house rules and women were off limits during TCCB hours. The TCCB expected the captain of England to deport himself in accordance with the status of his office. There was an undercurrent of snobbery in practically every utterance from May and the TCCB on this issue; a sense that this was the sort of thing that happens when you put a chap from a secondary modern in charge of a cricket team – that these oiks simply don't know how to behave. We all know what the Establishment thinks Gatting should have done. He should have retired to his room with a good claret and toasted marshmallows over an open fire in the company of a young chorister and none of this fuss would have happened.

His successor was May's godson, Chris Cowdrey (Tonbridge School) – an appointment that stank of the malign influence of the old-boy network. So even as late as 1988, some twenty years after the professional/amateur barriers had been removed, it was evident that English cricket had still not rid itself of the shackles of amateurism and snobbery.

Publicly humiliated when his second coming as captain was refuted by TCCB mandarin, Ossie Wheatley, in 1989, Gatting turned his back on the Test arena and pig-headedly took a team of sorry-looking rebels to South Africa. He was a pivotal figure in what had been a running sore for English cricket ever since the D'Oliveira Affair. It was an ignominious period for a self-confessed patriot whose actions wrought havoc on the game that he loved. Gatting returned to the England fold for the hapless 1992 tour of

India and was retained to counter the threat of leg-spinning prodigy, Shane Warne, in 1993. Gatting had a reputation for being the country's best player of spin, which made Warne's first ball in Test cricket on English soil all the more ironic. It pitched just outside leg stump and spun across the bat to hit the top of off. It was dubbed the ball of the century. The batsman? You guessed it.

On his final tour of Australia in 1995, Gatting exemplified the sorry state of English cricket. Seemingly immobile in the field, undone by pace, flummoxed by Warne, he was a clapped-out old banger that needed trading in for a newer model. As a Test player, Gatting never fulfilled his potential (av. 35.55) and unsure of himself in the Test arena his batting was characterised by a hesitancy and introspection rarely evident in his batting for Middlesex. His hamfistedness in matters of politics and race mirrored that of the authorities and his constant reselection for England when he was way past his prime betrayed the English obsession with the tried and trusted over youth. The career of this Falstaffian figure draws together the various neuroses that have bedevilled English cricket during my lifetime and with him now a selector, we can only hope that both he and the cricket authorities will learn from the mistakes of the past.

Supporting England is undoubtedly a test of faith. All those hours of self-neglect in front of the TV set, living off tins of Boddingtons and chocolate Hobnobs, peeing into the yukka plant because you daren't leave the room and risk the fall of a wicket, the all-night vigils shouting abuse at Charles Colvile, and standing outside Curry's in the drizzle peering through the shop window and willing England to hold on for a draw as the last bus home pulls away. All of this sacrifice for such rare and paltry rewards. But then

I sometimes wonder how dull it would have been to be a Jamaican during the eighties or an Australian in the nineties, wiping the floor with everybody and carrying all before you. We would all have missed out on that most numbing of white-knuckle rides, the ride that has been known to make grown men weep – 'The England Cricket Team Experience'. And if you've had your eyes shut over the last two decades on the rollercoaster of English cricket, here's an A–Z guide to remind you of the worst bits of life as an England cricket supporter.

A – ACADEMY (AUSTRALIAN)
How could anyone forget that heady weekend on the last tour of Australia when England lost twice to a team that didn't own a razor between them? Maybe there's something in this stubble business after all.

B – BLEWETT SYNDROME
A recently identified medical condition common among England supporters. Symptoms include nausea and feelings of depression and is brought on when young, wet-behind-the-ears debutants take the piss out of the England bowling. Similar condition to Azharuddinitis, named after the young Indian batsman who scored three centuries in his first three Tests.

C – CORPORATE ENTERTAINMENT
Otherwise known as twelve blokes in blue blazers and cream chinos getting plastered on cheap Chilean wine and talking about the Nikkei Index all day. It's because of these twats that you have to book your Test match tickets in October.

D – DICKIE
A fluffy white cloud floats into view and Dickie gets his

lightmeter out. No day at the cricket is complete without the full Dickie Bird performance. A scratch of the head, a look at the sky, a fidget, a look at the meter, a consultation with the other umpire, a shake of the head, a chat with the batsmen and . . . bingo! They're off. Then, Dickie slips out of his coat and returns to the middle in slacks and cricket jumper, arms folded, for about three hours waiting for it to start raining. You've paid £32 for the seat plus the grub and the travelling, you should be doing your nut. But bizarrely, a Dickie Day is often a lot less stressful than watching England bat.

E – ERNIE
Many of you may think that ERNIE (Electronic Random Number Indicator Equipment) is the thing they use to pick the premium bond winners, but I am able to reveal to you exclusively that it is also the system used by the England cricket selectors. How else do you think J.P.Stephenson or J.P.Taylor got picked? They even have the same serial codes.

F – FLETCHER
We should have known what was in store for us when he dropped those slip catches at Headingley on his debut. Was he called 'Gnome' because of his appearance or because he held out his bat like gnomes hold fishing rods?

G – GROUND REGULATIONS
No more than four tins of alcohol each, no sitting on the boundary edge, no banners, no singing, no horns, no drums, no making any noise . . . in fact, no bloody atmosphere!

H – HEMMINGS
'He's fat, he's round, you can slog him out the ground,

Eddie Hemmings, Eddie Hemmings.' Just one simple question: why?

I – INJURIES (AND ILLNESSES)
No other team seems to get injuries like ours. Pringle famously pulled a muscle writing a letter. Nobody understood how he could do this at the time, but now that we've read his pieces in the *Independent* over the last few years, we can imagine the contorted position he has to get his body into in order to fill his column. Chris Lewis' medical history runs to volumes, while Devon Malcolm got chicken pox for God's sake on the eve of the first Test against Australia in 1994. You can bet your life that if the Bubonic plague returned to these shores, the England cricket team would be the first to go down with it.

J – JUNE
'Oh to be in England in June!' Tennis at Wimbledon, racing at Royal Ascot, the Henley Regatta, and England 3–0 down in the series. A typical English summer.

K – KEITH (OR POSSIBLY, KEVIN)
This is the bloke who always sits behind you at Test matches. He has his clipboard and coloured pens and will dutifully record every detail of the day's play. Unfortunately, he will also listen to *Test Match Special* and publicly reveal every utterance made by Bill Frindall during the day – 'That partnership of 27 is the highest ninth-wicket partnership by a Sri Lankan pair at Lord's.' This man is not so much an anorak as a cagoule.

L – LEVER
With bowling coaches like Peter, who needs enemies? At a time when Devon Malcolm, England's potential match-winner, was having his confidence and action systematically destroyed, we sat at home and watched Paul Adams

run through our top order with deliveries that seemed to emanate from his armpit. If only Peter could have worked on his action.

M – MAY
The month that ushers in summer. A month of hope and expectation as we look forward to the season ahead, reading the player profiles of the touring party, picking our eleven for the first Test. Unfortunately, the other May, Peter, is doing the same and he's got his godson down as captain.

N – NEW ZEALAND
The heart sinks when you realise New Zealand are touring. Your mind goes back to all those dreary contests watching Vic Pollard, Bruce Edgar, John Wright, Jeremy Coney, and now Blair Pocock grinding their way to a five-hour 30. Or bowlers like Ewan Chatfield, Martin Snedden, Chris Pringle or Gavin Larsen trundling in for hours on end. We all know a Test series against New Zealand works quicker than a pint of Night Nurse with a whisky chaser.

O – ONE-CAP WONDERS
Who's your favourite? Alan Wells – 14 years waiting for his chance and then a first baller? Or, Andy Lloyd getting pole-axed by Malcolm Marshall? Or, Neil Williams getting the call-up and being told by Micky Stewart he was actually England's 17th choice seamer? Who will be the next lucky winner of the Lord's Lotto?

P – PRINGLE
In 1987, before they found themselves together at the helm of English cricket, Ray Illingworth and Keith Fletcher were chatting in India about the forthcoming World Cup. Ever loyal, Fletcher opined that Derek Pringle could be England's banker in the tournament. 'You did say "banker"?' Illy

asked, seeking clarification. England supporters had known the truth for some time.

Q – QUEEN'S PARK OVAL (TRINIDAD)
See Chapter 7.

R – RAIN
When was the last time rain saved England? And yet be it in Trinidad in 1990 when rain, bad light and Desmond Haynes' go-slow contrived to deny England an unassailable 2–0 lead in the series, or in Sydney in 1994 when rain, bad light, and the umpires calling the game off too soon thwarted a probable victory, or even in South Africa when rain ruined the Pretoria and Durban Tests with England in the box seat, we always seem to get the raw end of the deal.

S – STRAWS (CLUTCHING AT)
See R – Rain (above).

T – TAILENDERS
Carl Rackemann batting for over an hour against Tufnell and Hemmings in 1991 at Adelaide; Waqar Younis steering Pakistan home at Lord's in 1992; Warne and May resisting England's push at Sydney in 1995; Paul Adams tonking Devon about in Cape Town in 1996; and Danny Morrison saving the match with Nathan Astle at Auckland in 1997. If you know of a more cruel form of torture, then answers on a postcard to: Amnesty International (England Cricket Section).

U – UMPIRES
Darrell Hair twice not calling for a TV replay in 1994–95. Bulawayo umpires Messrs Dunne and Robinson not calling wides in the final overs. Shakoor Rana. (See also Straws, Clutching at.)

V – VICTORY (OVERSEAS)
Christchurch and Wellington in 1992 and 1997. Barbados in 1994. Adelaide in 1995. Do you remember what we're talking about now?

W – WARNE
The most exciting talent in modern cricket who has lifted the art of leg-spin bowling to new levels? Or, an arrogant fat beach bum who should sod off back to Bondi and leave our blokes alone? These two responses differentiate the lover of cricket from the wretched England cricket supporter.

X – X CERTIFICATE
Any video recording of:
Devon groping at Warne's hat-trick ball.
Marsh and Taylor batting all day at Trent Bridge in 1989.
The last day at Lord's in 1984 when Gower had the temerity to declare against West Indies and Greenidge and Gomes blasted 344 in just over four hours to win.
Ian Greig and Derek Pringle in harness against Pakistan in 1982.
Actually most of the Test matches since 1971.

Y – YORKSHIRE
Let's just add Lumb, Stevenson, Bairstow, Moxon, Blakey and Jarvis to that list of ours earlier.

Z – ZIMBABWE
Eight full-time professionals, just two teams in its domestic first-class cricket structure, and about 150 registered club players but still we get skittled for 118 by a chicken farmer.

I have to believe that I am a better person for having witnessed all of this, that it has enabled me to take a more balanced view of the world and my own tiny place in it, and that I have now acquired the strength to cope with anything fate might throw at me.

Oh sod it! What's the number for the Samaritans?

CHAPTER THREE

A Class Act
School cricket
and class politics

Crump House v Sir William Borlase's Grammar School

Date: 28 June 1976   *Venue:* Crump House   *Toss*: Sir William Borlase

Sir William Borlase

M.Bussell	run out	16
G.Pearson	run out	27
† T.Coombes	run out	3
S.Foster	run out	8
* M.Storey	not out	32
I.Robinson	run out	29
R.Faul	lbw b Cassells	7
P.Craven	lbw b Lambert	2
G.Rawlinson	not out	2
Extras		11

Total (7 wickets)   137

Bowling	O	M	R	W
Farmer	6	1	31	0
Joseph	4	0	27	0
Roach	4	0	17	0
Lambert	5	0	28	1
Cassells	3.4	0	23	1

Match Abandoned – Rain.

I went to one of those all-boys' grammar schools that was in all but name and resources a public school. It had all the trappings of a public school. Masters wore gowns and mortar boards, cloisters built when the school was founded in 1664 led to ancient, decaying classrooms, and homosexuality was rampant in the fifth form.

Everywhere you went you were reminded of its history. Mary Shelley's cottage where she wrote *Frankenstein* stood in the school grounds. Sepia photographs of masters and boys in sensible haircuts and shoes the shape of Fangio's Ferrari lined the cloister walls. There were open-top desks covered with graffiti through the ages from 'Rex loves Vera Lynn' to 'Ozzy Osbourne is King'. Paintings of old Borlase himself and the lineage of headmasters hung in the lobby of Old School House. This was the inner sanctum of the school where the headmaster had his study under the staff room and secretarial offices. If you were in Old School House you were there for one of two reasons. Either you were having one of the headmaster's mutually congratulatory chats over tea and Bourbon biscuits about your successful but unexceptional exam results, or you were being grilled as to what you knew about the recent razing of the groundsman's hut or the kidnapping of the music master. The little chats with the headmaster were always hysterical. He would ask you what your career plans were, to which, whatever you replied, he would then follow up with, 'Have you thought about the civil service?' You might have said you wanted to be an Arctic explorer or a rock star but he would always counter with the civil service option. We began to suspect he was on some backhander but subsequently learned to play a much more amusing game with him. The task was to come up with a chosen career so esoteric that even he could not just skate over it to discuss the civil service. We tried variously embalming, taxidermy and mammography, but a boy by the name of Summers hit the jackpot when he informed the headmaster that he desired to swell the ranks of the country's 'equine artificial insemination technicians'. The head fell for the bait. 'Equine wotnots . . . what's that exactly?' Summers had a free hand to reply and went for it: 'They jack off racehorses sir.'

Such moments helped you to steer a sane course through the mind-numbing, suffocating tedium of school life. It seemed to me in the seventies that when you walked through the school gate, you entered another world from another time. Outside it was Afghan coats, flared trousers, platform shoes, T Rex, Sweet, Wizzard, Ford Capris and free love. Inside it was black gowns, blazers and caps, the school hymn (with the catchy title *Te digna Sequere* or 'Follow Things Worthy'), Latin, bicycles and cold showers. The school was clinging on to the values of a bygone age and its practices and institutions seemed anomalous to every one of us. We were witnessing the slow death of a Victorian legacy.

The school had a strong sporting reputation, especially for rugby and in later years for hockey too. Cricket did not have the same profile. Athletics cut across the first part of the season and so cricket did not start in earnest until the first week of June. This left us just six Saturdays and a handful of 30-over-a-side thrashes on a Wednesday afternoon/evening. Our sports master was Alan Black, who played lock forward for Wasps, South-East Counties, and England 'B'. Standing 6ft 4in Bill McLaren would doubtless have called him a 'mobile lighthouse' and chortle about 'not wanting to bump into him down a dark alley'. Known by everyone as 'Bonehead' behind his back and 'Mr Black, sir' to his face, he terrified the shit out of us. But while he brought an expertise to rugby training and filled the school display cabinet with silverware, he knew about as much about cricket as . . . well, Charles Colvile.

To be fair to Black (well, he *is* 6ft 4in) he didn't try to hide his complete ignorance about cricket and so once we reached the age of fifteen we were coached by other masters who liked the game and knew where gully stood. But for three years all pupils received their cricketing education from the Alan Black Academy. 'Spread out in a ring,' he would command the fielders, 'and stop it if it comes near you. Here, you put these on,' thrusting the wicket-keeper's gloves at Mills. 'But I'm a fast bowler, sir.' 'Not today you're not,' Black would retort. The finer points of the game naturally passed him by. 'Don't bother with that fancy stuff, Bussell,' he instructed as I tried to impart some off-spin to the ball, 'just bowl it straight.' It could have been Keith Fletcher talking.

I was an enthusiastic player of moderate ability who, though I say it myself, compensated for this lack of natural talent with a studious array of defensive strokes. Most of the kids in those early lessons with Bonehead were intent on smacking the cover off the ball. But this offended my sense of the subtlety of the game. I was far more concerned with perfecting an airtight forward defensive lunge. This immediately cast me in a role as opening batsman – a part I was to play for many years. The other kids played with a swashbuckling abandon and scored breezy 20s and 30s before the law of averages dictated they would miss a heave at a straight one. On the other hand, I was renowned for compiling gritty and painstaking 8s until Black would threaten me with a cross-country run if I didn't get myself out. But I knew that sooner or later these kids would have to learn to play cricket the proper way – well, the English way at least. For cricket coaching in England is all about taking boys who with an instinctive eye can swat the ball high, wide and handsome over cow corner and beating these eccentricities out of them in pursuit of an orthodox technique. Not until they can play in the prescribed manner with straight bats and high left elbows are the nation's coaches happy. Nobody scores any runs but those elbows look lovely. And if you doubt this, just recall the outcry at the way Mark Lathwell and more recently Alistair Brown approached batting at international level.

Mr Welch, the history master, took charge of cricket in the fifth form. He had been a decent club player in his time and though well into his fifties could still bowl nippy away cutters. He had a neurotic obsession with neatness in the field. 'A tidy team plays tidy cricket' was his motto and it seemed the neat and efficient ferrying of the ball from wicket-keeper to bowler via gully, cover and mid-off was what really gave him pleasure on a cricket field. We could have been bowled out for 25 and hammered by 10 wickets but if we hadn't dropped a catch getting the ball back to the bowler he seemed quite happy.

The etiquette of cricket was also right at the top of his agenda. He disliked fielders shining the ball on their trousers. Only the bowler was allowed to do this and then only for a maximum of three rubs since it was considered impolite to keep the batsman waiting. Furthermore, only the bowler and the wicket-keeper were allowed to appeal for LBWs as he tried to prove with geometric charts that no other fielder could have any geometric basis for an appeal.

Old Welch would not put up with the wardances from third slip that take place these days when ball strikes pad in front; rather he would have referred him to a basic geometry text book. In one match the boy Mills made the mistake of appealing from fine leg and Welch quivered incandescent with rage before barking loudly, 'Not out'. The rest of the over was played out in silence with fielders imploding with laughter behind turned backs and heaving shoulders. Mills was dropped for the remainder of the season for this effrontery.

The 1st and 2nd XIs were marshalled by Mr Wedd, one of the English masters and head of the boarding house. He was a cricket and hockey fanatic and clearly the likes of Shakespeare, Milton and Dickens were a damned inconvenience which got in the way of the important matters of beating Aylesbury GS on a Saturday. To be a member of one of his teams was to join a club of the pampered elite and to become a recipient of all sorts of privileges. You were excused unnecessary homework – you can't bat with your head full of Shakespeare sonnets – you were allowed to skip off early from lessons to prepare for net practice and during lessons surreptitiously passed little notes that read: 'England 84–1. Amiss 48n.o.' To be a cricketer in Mr Wedd's English class was to be a kulak among serfs.

In the winter months Wedd would put the hockey team through its paces and draw up interminable cricket team lists as he sought to get the right blend for the 1st XI. Could Pearson be trusted to open the innings after his ugly cross-bat swipe at John Hampden School? Would Storey find his leg spinner again? Should Coombes keep wicket now that he was batting at number 3? Would Parker's dose of the clap clear up before the start of the season? These were the problems that exercised Wedd's mind. By May he would be like a dog on heat tethered outside a pet shop.

His wife, a rather large woman and unyielding in every imaginable way, had borne him one child – a daughter. We pictured him in bed lying next to his wife – who under blankets must have looked like a scale transection of the Atlas Mountains – plucking up courage to ask for her cooperation in producing the cricket-playing son he so obviously wanted. But I guess the sheer magnitude of the physical task in hand, even with ropes and a plentiful supply of Kendal mint cake, was just too daunting. So, instead, he was reduced to seeking vicarious sporting pleasure through his pupils.

But it is the season of 1976 in the U-16s under the tutelage of Mr Welch that we focus on – a turbulent season that saw no less than four different captains in six matches.

Robinson was far and away the best cricketer of my year. A solid middle-order batsman he also took the new ball and moved it through the air and off the pitch both ways. A hot-headed fellow, he was saddled most years with the burdens of captaincy, something for which he was psychologically completely unsuited. He would be guaranteed at least once a season to lose his rag on the field and he had been carpeted on many occasions by umpires both home and away. His most hysterical outburst came against Dr Challoner's GS in the same match that Mills had blotted his copy book with the appeal from fine leg. Robinson was batting smoothly and had got to 30-odd when he was sawn off in his prime by a ball that pitched about a foot outside the leg stump from a left arm over bowler. The finger of death was raised by the opposition umpire in response to the appeal, and Robinson was out. He looked at the umpire with incredulity: 'Out? How can that be out?!' 'It's out,' is all their stone-faced umpire would add to the debate. The rest of us started to hide all the dangerous looking bits of kit and remove all sharp objects from the pavilion. But Robinson was still standing his ground. 'You're out, Robinson,' came the command from Mr Welch at square leg, doggedly supporting his inept colleague. Robinson stared at Welch through mean eyes and then huffily put his bat under his arm and started his walk to the pavilion. For a moment we thought the volcano had been contained but then suddenly Robinson returned to the wicket and proceeded to pummel the pitch with a flat bat near the spot he thought it had landed. 'I'd hate anybody else to get such a bad bounce,' he sneered and flounced off.

Mr Welch was blowing steam from his ears and we grappled with the prospect of a nuclear winter in the minibus back home. Needless to say, Robinson was relieved of the captaincy the following day and I was put in charge. Unlike Atherton or Gooch, though, whose batting positively flourished with the captaincy, mine fell apart like an MFI bookcase. As an opening batsman I became all the more obsessed with the need to post a decent score and my batting became all the more constipated. By my third match as captain, I was practically sculpted into the forward defensive position before the bowler had started his run up and after scoring 12 in 21 overs I was deliberately run out on Welch's instructions by Foster. Indeed, it was Foster who was to take over from me as captain in the next match after I had been told to go away and write down as many differences as I could think of between a batsman and a brick wall.

Foster was a lad of slight stature who brought to his cricket a small man's perspective of the world. He was not a short arse of the chippy aggressive sort who wants to invade Russia, just the type who cannot resist a challenge. This was just as well because his first match in charge was against RGS High Wycombe who in turn were led by a chap called Phil Newport. Phil, as we know, went on to play for Worcestershire and, like every bowler who stays in the first-class game long enough, England too. He never looked like making the grade at Test match level (10 wickets at 41.70), but at fifteen years old he was in a different stratosphere to the rest of us. Newport was one of those fifteen-year-olds who at 6ft 3in and 14 stones was a man among boys. He opened the batting and was awesome; latching on to anything fractionally short, leaning into drives with sumptuous timing, and playing off his legs. This is always the litmus test of quality. To a decent player, the leg-side half volley has four written all over it. At my level it has 'broken foot' written all over it. In twenty-odd years of playing I could count on the toes of Fred Titmus' feet the number of leg-side glides for four I have pulled off. But Newport punished anything on his legs. He made 80 out of 100 before he got bored and went for another huge six over the tennis courts and lost his leg stump. RGS batted competently but much less commandingly thereafter and scored 197 for seven before declaring and leaving us 80 minutes plus 20 overs to get them.

But if we thought Newport's batting was good, it took only two overs from him to prove to us that his bowling was brilliant and that they had set us about 150 more than they needed. His deliveries seamed, they swung, they bounced, and they smashed your stumps over. They were like heat-seeking missiles in their pinpoint accuracy. (Actually, that's not strictly true. If they had been heat-seeking missiles they would have homed in on the warm contents of our underpants rather than our middle stumps.) After just 15 balls we were 5 for three. I had watched the carnage from the safety of the other end, steadfastly refusing to risk a single and the prospect of facing a Newport Exocet. Captain Foster strode to the wicket with his chest puffed out, looking not unlike a mini Allan Border. I met him in the middle and was about to communicate the full horror of what was in store when he announced: 'I'm going to get down the track to him ... knock him off his length,' and with that turned to take guard. I was aghast. My jaw dropped. Much in the same way Foster's did, when, good to his word, he pranced down the wicket first ball and collected a lifter full square in the mandible. Foster was taken off to casualty for precautionary x-rays and Newport was taken off to avoid further injuries. The damage, however, was done. There's nothing quite like a pool of blood outside off stump to put the wind up a batting side and from then on our batting lasted only marginally longer than it takes a humming bird to sing 'Yankee Doodle Dandy'. Foster returned from casualty with a mouth like a giant pin cushion just in time to see us all out for 31 and we travelled home in humiliated silence in the minibus. Foster was dropped as captain for the next match against Crump House on the grounds that none of us could understand what he was saying.

There was always a bit of needle in our matches with Crump House, a private school that took boys up to the age of twelve or thirteen. I can't recall how it worked precisely but it was something along the lines of their 1st XI playing our U-15s and their 2nd XI playing our U-14s and so on. It basically meant that we were always playing against kids one year our junior and this rankled. But what was really at issue in this match against Crump was the hoary old subject of class.

Class seems irrelevant to most other sports. Football has traditionally been the preserve of the working classes and while this is being currently undermined by middle-class season ticket-holders and big business chasing the TV money, it has remained at its core the working man's game. Rugby resolved whatever tensions class caused by splitting into two codes. The flat cap and whippet brigade in the north playing rugby league, and the fedora and poodle crowd in the south continuing with rugby union. But cricket is still rather schizophrenic about class, the result of a clash between myth and reality.

The myth of blacksmith standing shoulder to shoulder with landowner in harmonious combat with their rivals on an English village green is an enduring one. But while cricket is, and always has been, played by all classes, it is, and always was, riven with prejudice and snobbery. When in the 1750s cricket developed into the game we recognise today, it was the first game played by the upper classes (and certainly the first one that did not involve a shotgun). Hitherto, the upper classes had merely seen sport as a spectacle, or a business, or a gambling medium. But if they were going to *play* the game, they were adamant they were going to control it. So, while the myth of blacksmith and landowner playing together remains, the reality is they did so only under the rules of the landowners. The laws of the game and the commercial basis on which matches were staged were prescribed by the landowners in a shambolic and haphazard way throughout the 18th century and early 19th century, until the MCC assumed governance of the game. The Marylebone Cricket Club was founded by an aristocratic elite to play cricket on privately owned land away from the unwashed hordes who flocked to matches played on common land. These principles have more or less remained intact ever since and though the club now leases its ground to Middlesex and allows the paying public to watch, the club itself is still very much an exclusive organisation that puts a premium on social background and having the right connections. For the well-being of the game to have been in the hands of the privileged elite for so long, is the main reason that cricket has been beset by so many class barriers. We do well to remember that in the sixties a rigid hierarchy based on social class (a hierarchy that was being dismantled in most other walks of life by a social revolution of sorts) existed in cricket which demanded separate dressing rooms, separate gates to the playing areas, and different forms of personal address among the players.

Yet if the MCC were the high priesthood of cricket elitism, the public schools were its missionaries. The striped cap and blazer, the haughty attitude, the cavalier batsmanship (for the hard work of bowling was always left to the labourers) symbolised a superiority that comes from the confidence of control and ownership. They were playing their game. And they were playing it under their rules. None of us understood this at the time but we instinctively took a dislike to the striped cap of Crump House. In fact, around the whole world a striped cap is a red rag to the most mild mannered of bowling bulls. Suddenly bowlers that were complaining only minutes ago about sore feet, or not wanting to bowl into the wind, are queuing up to knock that poncey cap off.

But back to the match with Crump House; a match that because of Mr Welch's attendance at an examiners' conference meant we came under the Svengali influence of Mr Wedd for the first time. For him it was a chance to cast his eye over his future charges, but more importantly, to get out of teaching Form 3a *The Rime of the Ancient Mariner*. Within minutes we noticed a difference between his thinking and that of Mr Welch. Welch wanted above all the game to be played in the right spirit. Wedd wanted to win at practically any cost.

'Now three rules,' Wedd chimed, as we pulled out of the school gates and started our journey to Crump House. 'One: look for quick singles. Nothing infuriates a team more than quick singles. Two: if it hits the pads for God's sake pipe up. It's the umpire's job to pass judgement, and your job to ask him.' If only Mills could have heard this. 'Thirdly, whatever you do, make a bloody din doing it. I want to hear you shout for a run, shout your appeals, and grunt when you're bowling. A noisy team is a winning team.' His motto could not have been more different. Whether he really believed any of this was irrelevant. Its effect was to instill confidence. We had a gameplan: to get up the noses of the opposition. For the first time that season we were a team with a common purpose, not eleven cowering individuals terrified of besmirching the good name of cricket by some appalling social gaffe.

On arrival at the school with its imposing Gothic buildings and well-maintained grounds, we were met by a Mr Richardson who was Crump's master in charge of cricket. He and Wedd knew each other from their days together on the Bucks schools hockey committee.

'Hello, Wedd. You found us OK then?'

'Fine.'

'Did you come by public transport? I didn't see a coach,' Richardson goaded.

'Minibus actually,' Wedd bristled. 'It's gone on to drop the swimmers off at the gala.'

'Jolly good. Now how about 25 overs a side? Do you think you chaps can last out 25 overs?'

'Oh, we've got all evening. But what time do your lot have to be tucked up in bed?'

Touché. And round one to Mr Wedd we all thought. This match was always going to be about much more than just cricket. It was about class – public school versus grammar school. Two conflicting but elitist views of the world – one based on exclusiveness by academic achievement, the other exclusiveness based on money, and both Wedd and Richardson wanted to prove a point.

Crump House won the toss and invited us to bat on a perfectly manicured wicket on a glorious but muggy summer's afternoon. It was a picture from Constable or a scene from a Merchant Ivory film. The thatched pavilion, the window boxes full of blooming azaleas, the chapel peeping over the oak trees to one side of the ground, the lush emerald green pasture rolling away into the valley the other side. This was an England of holiday brochures. An England for which old soldiers had fought in the muddy fields of Flanders. An England without motorway service stations, and tramps clutching bottles of Woodpecker in plastic bags, and Bob Monkhouse.

I walked out to bat to a hearty cry of 'Batsman in' from the Crump captain and polite applause. I took guard, surveyed the field and settled over my bat mentally rehearsing my forward lunge. I had played this shot to the first ball of every innings since I was ten and I saw no reason to change now. The ball propitiously clunked into my bat and dropped at my feet. 'Yes!' Pearson, my opening partner boomed, remembering Wedd's instructions about short singles and making a racket, and we scampered home without alarm. I was amazed. This was a cricketing road to Damascus for me. If I could turn the forward prod into a source of runs there could be no stopping me. I could be into double figures before dusk. Pearson nicked the next ball into his pads and I called him through for another quick single, made all the easier by Pearson kicking the ball past the swooping bowler as he set off for the run. We ticked along like this for a few overs until the ring of fielders was so close you could hear them breathe. That's when I unleashed my drive over the top. Truth be told it was (and is still) more of a defensive prod with a sudden flourish but it provoked ecstatic cheers from my teammates outside the pavilion as it cleared mid-off and we scurried through for two. Crump were at sixes and sevens. Their captain was ball chasing – putting a fielder wherever the last runs had been scored – bowlers sniped at their fielders, overthrows were commonplace, and Richardson was hissing with rage at his young blades.

At 38 for nought off seven overs we were cruising and Mr Wedd had a beatific smile across his face. At 52 for four after four run outs going for unlikely singles, the smile had turned to a scowl. Robinson and Storey put the innings back on a stable footing with a partnership of over 40 when Robinson skied a catch to mid-wicket. He let out a scream of 'Yes, one!!', as a quaking Crump fielder positioned himself under the steepling catch, and continued to yell like a banshee as he set off for the second run. The fielder didn't lay a hand on it, the ball going straight through outstretched fingers that could have been winding imaginary wool, hit his chest and squirted away allowing Robinson to complete three. Wedd beamed. Richardson was not so pleased. He walked down the wicket and spoke sternly to Robinson.

'Anything the matter?' Wedd enquired.

'I'm just warning your boy about ungentlemanly conduct – all that hollering.'

'Nothing wrong with loud, clear calling, is there?'

The match resumed but war had now broken out between the masters. Robinson was upbraided by Richardson for running on the pitch. Wedd informed Crump's best bowler that he was very close to being no-balled for chucking. He was advised to straighten his arm at all times during the delivery which had the desired effect on his bowling, as he began spraying it about everywhere. The scoreboard ticked over nicely, although Robinson was the fifth run out of the match, but by now we boys were mere pawns in a much broader battle between the two masters. The turning down of a plumb LBW appeal was countered with a spate of 'one-short' signals from Richardson. Dodgy LBW decisions from Richardson provoked a series of wide calls from Wedd to balls that shaved the leg stump. But as black storm clouds skudded overhead to match the mood of the match, the game moved on to a higher level of skulduggery.

Storey went tripping down the wicket to meet a well-flighted off-spinner that dipped and turned past the inside edge and nestled into the gloves of Crump's wicket-keeper. He was stumped by a mile. In fact so far was he out of his ground that Storey didn't even bother to look round and, with the first spots of leaden rain now falling, he dragged himself away from the wicket. Wicket-keeper and bowler were congratulating themselves and other fielders were approaching the happy couple when from nowhere a cry of 'No ball!' was heard. The whole world seemed to stop. Bowler and wicket-keeper looked at each other. Storey turned round. And fielders searched to find the source of this confident bellow. There was Wedd standing at square leg, arm outstretched. Richardson was nonplussed.

'No ball, Mr Wedd?'

'No ball, Mr Richardson. I'm afraid your wicky took the ball in front of the stumps. Great pity because he was a long way out of his ground. No ball, scorer. Back here, Storey.'

The *coup de grâce* had been delivered. There weren't many rules left to bend and perhaps for the good of future relations between the schools, the big spots of rain soon turned into a thunderstorm of tropical proportions. The match was abandoned after a tea which put the Borlase equivalent of a cup of squash and a stale doughnut to shame. Everyone shook hands and Wedd and Richardson talked heartily of a good contest played in a good competitive spirit. A little vignette of the English class system had just been played out and as we showered and changed, we felt we'd at least given the toffs a bloody nose, if not the broken one we'd wanted to.

'We must do this again, Wedd,' boomed Richardson, shaking his hand.

'Absolutely, can't wait,' our man replied.

And they both parted presumably planning on how they could introduce trip wires, land mines, and mustard gas into the next encounter. We clambered into the minibus and Wedd fired up the old diesel guzzler but within seconds we knew we'd been trumped. Our nearside rear tyre had been let down. It proved once again you should never trust a toff.

CHAPTER FOUR

Sex, Lies and Sheepdip
Village cricket in the raw

Radnage v Bledlow Ridge

Date: 9 August 1980   *Venue:* Radnage Common

Radnage

G.Breslaw	c Vernon b Newell	28
R.Wilson	b Collier	16
M.Seals	run out	16
M.Bussell	b Carter	39
C.Barker	c Carter b Horne	44
I.Rutter	b Newell	0
R.Howarth	b Newell	0
* P.Redman	c Shine b Horne	17
J.Boden	c&b Horne	6
† E.Stephenson	c Brooks b Collier	3
C.Parry	not out	5
Extras		5
Total		179

Bowling	O	M	R	W
Newell	10	1	44	3
Collier	10.2	0	41	2
Horne	8	0	37	3
Carter	4	0	29	1
Tombs	4	2	11	0
Merryweather	3	1	12	0

Bledlow Ridge

†* B.Brooks	lbw b Rutter	22
A.Carter	b Barker	29
J.Tombs	b Redman	41
C.Carter	c Breslaw b Boden	11
M.Brooks	c Redman b Boden	5
R.Vernon	c Parry b Boden	13
D.Shine	c&b Wilson	2
P.Merryweather	b Barker	0
E.Horne	not out	7
C.Newell	c Barker b Redman	1
L.Collier	c Howarth b Barker	14
Extras		22
Total		167

Bowling	O	M	R	W
Redman	9	0	29	2
Boden	11	1	46	3
Barker	7	1	34	3
Rutter	7	0	28	1
Wilson	3	0	8	1

There are two images of village cricket. The first is that favoured by TV executives and John Major's speech writers and is unfurled for us in soft focus – balmy summer's afternoons, with the wholesome sound of willow on leather, the cry of 'Come one' as Mr Ingleby-Challinor, who lives in the old manor house, plays a feudal cover drive off the bowling of Jenks, the local dairy farmer, towards the verger who fields it in prescribed fashion on one knee. Everyone then retires to The Three Feathers, a local hostelry, whose frothing ales are consumed to much merriment. There, old Harry, who singlehandedly liberated Rangoon, leads the snug bar in a chorus of 'The Eton Boating Song'.

The reality, however, is somewhat different. Mr Ingleby-Challinor has no time for cricket since he converted his manor house into a conference centre hosting sales away-days for executives in Sierras. Farmer Jenks is too busy feeding his EU subsidised herd its grandparents' organs. And the verger, having been caught in the organ loft playing chopsticks wearing nothing but a bikini, is otherwise engaged negotiating an exclusive with the *News of the World*. Meanwhile, old Harry, who is a curmudgeonly old soak and hasn't bought a round since the Queen's Silver Jubilee, plays Pacman in The Tudor Barne (the pub-cum-steakhouse that used to be The Three Feathers) with the location crew shooting *When Lovers Meet*, the BBC's new costume drama. Instead, on the field of play, Vince, a medical supplies rep, is using his mobile phone to report the home side to the league for preparing a sub-standard pitch and insisting they be docked the statutory points.

When I was sixteen my family uprooted from Marlow and moved twelve miles to the tiny village of Radnage on the Oxfordshire border. My mother, in particular, had tired of suburbia and hankered after the country life. She wanted the full rural bit – the ivy-clad cottage, the paddock, the two wet labradors steaming in front of the Aga. I was much less taken by the rural idyll. The move came at an awkward stage in my development – an age when sixteen-year-old boys need a certain amount of freedom and independence to make prats of themselves away from the reproachful gaze of their parents. But now I was miles from school, miles from my friends, and completely beholden to my parents for lifts to and from what we called 'the action'.

'The action' largely consisted of us trying to get served in one of Marlow's thirty-odd pubs. So on Friday nights gaggles of youths from my school exchanged school uniform for a denim one and with our faces bound together by pustulating acne and sporting wispy Ronald Coleman moustaches, we would endeavour to convince sceptical landlords that we were over eighteen. On the rare occasions that we were admitted, we would stand at the bar ogling, but never daring to talk to, the local beauties and drinking vast quantities of lager top until one of our number either fell over or threw up in someone's scampi in a basket. On eviction, we would then seek much-needed ballast at the late-night chippie before staggering home to our parents with carefully crafted and entirely bogus accounts of a pleasant evening playing ping pong and drinking ginger beer down the youth club. Well, that's what I used to do, but after the move to Radnage I now had to suffer the humiliation of being met by my father at a predetermined place and time so that I could get a lift home.

In an attempt to retain some teenage dignity in the face of this parental mollycoddling, I would tell my mates that I was hitching back home which scored highly on the street credibility barometer but made the risk of discovery all the more terrifying. Each week I would change the rendezvous with my father as we played out a scene straight out of a thirties gangster 'B' movie: a shadowy figure moves stealthily, his back to the perimeter wall. He stops, looks left and then right, strokes his thin but rather fetching moustache and decides the coast is clear. Then he darts towards the waiting car, jumps into the back seat and barks at his chauffeur, 'Step on it, Dad. Let's get out of here.'

Mum threw herself into the country bit, joining the local branch of the Women's Institute, doing the flowers at the church, and buying a pedigree German pointer called Fritz. Eventually, she became president of the WI and was asked to join the parish council, but Fritz was markedly less of a success. Fritz ate everything. He ate us out of house and home – quite literally. For this neurotic beast would eat anything except dog food. Carpets, door mats, shoes, newspapers – this was Fritz's staple diet with unfortunate consequences at the other end of the digestive process. Believe me, the sight of a dog passing his lunch of half a loo mat and a size eleven moccasin is, as spectacles go, right down there with watching Bernard Manning go-go dancing in his birthday suit. But when Fritz started trying to eat next door's sheep, he had to go.

My father acquired a trilby, shooting stick and various other horsey accoutrements and went racing whenever possible while my brother took up riding at the local stables and would disappear at weekends to go hacking on some moth-eaten old nag who could doubtless see the glue factory looming large. I, meanwhile, joined the village cricket team with whom I was to play off and on for the next eight years. This was to open my eyes to real village life; not the James Herriot life the rest of my family were living out, but (if you'll excuse the alliteration) the patchwork of pettinesses, politics and prejudices of rural life.

Radnage is not what you might consider a picture postcard village. There is no village green ringed with thatched cottages, no village shop, no duckpond, no bearded blacksmith hammering away at a shire horse's hoof to be seen for miles. Instead, it is a handful of connected lanes flanked by tall hedgerows with two pubs about three miles apart and a common tucked between fields of rape and a small pre-war housing estate. Its unattractiveness does mean, though, that it has not been swamped by commuting stockbrokers or London-based weekenders. It is by and large still a farming community and upmarket dormitory for the local tradesmen of High Wycombe, traditionally from the furniture, paper milling and printing businesses. What it lacked in picturesque charm, however, it made up for in character. It was always a treat to see visiting ramblers drop by The Crown, the pub nearest the cricket ground, for their restorative halves of shandy. They must have felt they had walked on to the set of *Deliverance*. There was a turkey farmer who wore a ten-gallon hat and had a wooden leg; two brothers who lived in a caravan but hadn't exchanged a word with each other for over twenty years and sat scowling at each other from opposite ends of the pub; a builder who was often drunk and liked to quote chunks of *Das Kapital* to you; a man with a toupee that flapped every time the door opened and made the pub dog bark; and a farm labourer who had lost a finger in a threshing accident with the somewhat unfortunate result that his tattooed knuckles now bore the words 'Love' and 'Hat'.

This was also the village where the vicar shuttled between the three churches in his parish on a moped, his shoulder-length hair flowing out from under his helmet; where a dairy farmer had been arrested and subsequently imprisoned for devoting three acres of arable land to the growing of marijuana plants; and where two horrific murders had taken place within three years of each other, the latter involving a man decapitating his wife with a hatchet, burying her body in the garden and mounting her head on the television. Frankly, Radnage made *Emmerdale* with its incest and airplane crashes look like Toytown.

The members of Radnage Cricket Club did much to colour and characterise these wider village idiosyncracies. The club had for some years languished among the also-rans of the Mid-Bucks League but in the summer after my 'A' levels when I joined – and I would not want to understate the sheer coincidence – the team performed above everyone's expectations and finished third in the league. We were for that one year, and for no obvious reason, a team in the true sense of the word, rather than a collection of eleven churlish, disaffected, backstabbing individuals. Credit for imposing, albeit briefly, some semblance of order and discipline on this unlikely mob had to go to Phil, our captain. Phil was a young man who had just turned thirty and taken over the family's road haulage business, but in his schooldays he had been a decent cricketer. Indeed, his school had entered him in a fast bowlers' competition that was designed to unearth the Fred Truemans (or Fred Truemen) of the future. Phil had got to the final sixteen who were then sent for intensive coaching at The Oval. He bowled left arm over with a high side-on action and was quick. Too quick on his day for this level of cricket. But he was wild with it. It may have been a polished classical action but the radar was decidedly wonky. Brian Statham's mantra of 'If he misses, I'll hit' was in Phil's case more likely to apply to second slip's kneecap than the stumps. One unplayable delivery would be followed by one unreachable one.

Sharing the new ball at the other end was Jeff. Mild mannered and softly spoken off the pitch, on it Jeff was like a volcano waiting to erupt. Cricket and the club meant everything to him. He was unemployed and so the weekend contests on the cricket field had a special meaning to Jeff – a chance to express himself and vent his frustrations. Every week he walked the four miles to home matches over hill and down dale in open-toed sandals and flared flannels from a bygone era still dirty from the previous week's heroics. With his gaunt features and long stringy hair parted in the middle, Jeff could have been a pilgrim searching for the Via Dolorosa or opening the bowling with Rasputin for the Minsk Second XI. He was all effort; huffing and puffing off an absurdly long run and then growling at batsmen before trudging back to his mark somewhere in Berkshire. His run was so long that cover fielders new to Jeff's bowling would make the mistake of moving in at the start of Jeff's run only to find they had reached the wicket before Jeff had.

These two were backed up by the 'all-rounders'. There was Bob, a British Airways pilot who batted correctly and bowled very slow away-swingers to a packed offside field. Sound tactics so long as you didn't bowl all six deliveries down the legside as Bob was unfortunately prone to do. 'Chunky' (why, I never did find out) Barker, who had a face like a chipped Toby jug and a wonderful dry wit delivered in a slow Bucks drawl, bowled a brisk medium pace. 'All right, my precious?' he would ask as his sour-faced wife took the tea things away. 'She thinks I call her "precious" as a form of endearment,' he muttered to me one afternoon. 'Actually it's because when she's lying next to me in bed in the half light she looks just like Precious MacKenzie, the Commonwealth weightlifter.'

Finally on the bowling front, there was myself who tried to bowl off-spin on grounds too small to penalise mishits and to batsmen who had absolutely no respect for slow bowling. Indeed, I have found it to be an indisputable fact that the more sophisticated the level of cricket, the more unjustified respect the slow bowler gets. I have bowled maiden after maiden to decent club players who see demons in the most innocuous of deliveries and pat back half-volley after half-volley, and been smashed out of sight by various pig farmers who wouldn't recognise an arm ball if it stood up and gave them a whopping great EU subsidy.

The batting centred on a young lad called Graham, who went on to sign professional football forms with first Lincoln City and then Southend. Graham was one of those blokes who took the opportunity that changing into sports kit provided of strutting naked around the dressing room and all without a trace of self-consciousness. It must be said, it was an imposing sight and his manhood was memorably described by Chunky as 'like a toddler's arm clutching a tangerine' but it was bad for team morale, especially for those batsmen waiting to go in. It was hard enough shutting out from the mind the myriad of self doubts and deficiencies about your batting technique without this all too visible reminder of your physical inadequacies, as your own walnut whip quivered with apprehension under your abdomenal protector.

Malcolm, a plasterer by trade, batted at three. Malcolm's great talent was for running his own men out. Batting with him was a Russian roulette experience – you just never knew when he would go off on another suicidal single and so it was always with some selfish relief when Malcolm was dismissed (and exalted joy if he was run out). Our most destructive batsman was Ian, a lugubrious butcher who wielded his bat at weekends as he did his cleaver on weekdays. If the mood took him and luck went his way, he could turn a match in a handful of overs. Dealing only in fours and sixes, Ian was the 'hitman'. But it was always 'shit or bust'. Failure was a heavy burden he carried all week. A first-ball duck would see him slope off to his Avenger where he would seek solace with the sad, lonely and deranged on his CB radio. Back-to-back ducks over the weekend and you always feared he would be found by his colleagues on Monday morning hanging from a meat hook in the freezer.

The rest of the team was made up of chaps who probably should not have been in the team, but if they hadn't, there would not have been a club. Dick, the club's treasurer, could neither bat nor bowl but was a willing volunteer to field at short leg. Eddie, the fixture secretary and wicket-keeper, was a Welsh GP in his mid-fifties who in the dim and distant past had (as he frequently reminded us) played a decent level of cricket, keeping wicket on several occasions to the Glamorgan and England paceman Jeff Jones. And finally, Colin, the eternal cricketing optimist. He may not have been blessed with talent, but he had great faith that the next match would be the one he got his fifty and five-wicket haul. He was a sucker for new developments in bats – scoops, jumbos, double scoops, powerspots, Colin had tried them all. When I first met him he had just purchased one of those bats Lance Cairns used. It was a sort of club with sloping edges, more like a baseball bat in fact. I think the scientific thinking behind the design was that the new shape enhanced the hitting zone and made the edges weaker. Hence, the manufacturers believed, nicks were less likely to carry to fielders. What Colin had failed to appreciate, however, was that 99 per cent of his runs came from nicks so this bat rendered him practically impotent. He persisted though and there were seven straight ducks from Colin before we found the bat horribly disfigured in a bin outside the pub. Ever cheery, he bounced back the following week unveiling his new 'Magnum', a great railway sleeper of a bat that he believed would transform his game. A bad workman may blame his tools, but a bad batsman just goes out and buys a new bat.

The kit addict with his mistaken notion that the latest equipment can make up for a total absence of ability, is one of the sorrier sights in amateur sport. In his less than illustrious career Colin must have spent hundreds of pounds funding his belief that the new Gunn & Moore or a set of batting gloves with a big padded index finger is all that stands between him and a fifty. And that's what drove Colin to buy a helmet – not the fear of being hit on the head (he had played thirty years without such an injury), it was the belief that the helmet would somehow transform him into a better player. The consequences, however, were quite different. Frankly, it would have been cheaper and easier to paint target rings on his forehead. The helmet seemed to act as an invitation to all bowlers to pepper him with bouncers and beamers and it took three direct hits to the bean before we convinced Colin that he should go back to his wide-brimmed (with anti-glare lining) David Gower sunhat, if only for the sake of his health.

Colin did all those jobs without which no club could survive. He built the scoreboard, made the boundary markers, transported the team kit and also acted as unpaid groundsman. Week in week out, despite all his love and attention, he produced a typical village cricket wicket. Located on a slope, at the lower end where it took longer to drain, it hardly got up above ankle height, whereas at the drier top end it spat at you off a length and parted your hair down the middle. The wicket could certainly boast an impressive CV of smashed teeth, broken noses, cut eyes, and a host of bruised fingers.

It was always at its most lethal the day after the village fête. Twenty-four hours earlier the square had typically played host to among other things a bouncy castle, a cake stall, and a less than riveting display by the police dog-handlers. Dog after dog would clamber over walls, jump through hoops or wrestle with a policeman improbably disguised as a burglar wearing a black polo neck, a mask, and a pair of oven gloves. Spectators cooed and clapped at these tricks, but with a trowel and bucket at the ready Colin looked on, a picture of misery. It all played havoc with Colin's wicket and when one year the fête took place in constant drizzle and on a wet square, Colin finally flipped his lid. At the end of the fête Gypsy Rose's husband (Mr Nish) parked his Fiat Panda on the wicket to load up the fortune teller's tent, and tyre marks could be seen right across the square. Colin could not contain himself. He threatened to do something very nasty to Mr Nish with an unclaimed coconut. This sort of talk was asking for trouble, particularly when you consider it was directed at a man armed with a tent-peg mallet. An ugly incident ensued involving the said mallet, one bottle of Bailey's (won in the bottle raffle) and a Battenburg cake (purchased from the fête stall), which judging from her subsequent screaming our amateur fortune teller had clearly not seen coming.

Colin's cut head the following day told one part of the story, as did the puddle of Bailey's Irish cream and the marzipan crumbs on the wicket. It was all reminiscent of Headingley in 1975 when people protesting the innocence of London crook George Davis poured oil on the pitch and dug small holes on a length. After much deliberation, Ian Chappell, the Australian captain, refused to play on the damaged pitch or indeed an adjoining one. The match was abandoned and Australia retained the Ashes. It was anyone's guess how our opponents, Lacey Green, and their captain would view the large sticky stain caused by a coffee liqueur just outside the off stump. It would certainly have made for an interesting pitch report for the BBC's turfmeister Geoff Boycott: 'Well, it's a good kreekit pitch is this. A bit in it for t'bowlers but equally runs in it for t'batsmen who are prepared to get their 'eads down and graft like I used to. But if it don't turn, I'll be boogered. There's a popular coffee-flavoured nightcap 'ere and it's right on t'spinners' length.'

Like all groundsmen, though, Colin always thought the wicket would play better than it did. It had become, until his recent retirement, one of the summer's rituals to listen to former Headingley groundsman Keith Boyce declare on the eve of the Test match that the wicket he had prepared was an absolute belter and full of runs, only for the match to be all over by tea on the second day with some veteran trundler like Neil Mallender having been made to look like Dennis Lillee. Unlike Mr Boyce, Colin could be excused his pitches. He had kids playing football, youths on Lambrettas, and aggressive spouses of dodgy fortune tellers to cope with.

Elsewhere in our league the pitches may not have been in quite the same deathtrap category as ours, but the grounds certainly had their own eccentricities. At Bradenham, the small square is cut into a steep cross slope. It is perfectly flat but fielding in the outfield you don't so much need boots with spikes as ropes and crampons. It is almost impossible for batsmen to score a boundary up the hill and it is one of the more bizarre experiences I have had in the field to chase a ball and then find it rolling back towards me. Conversely, the merest of touches downhill would send the ball careering to the boundary and fielders stupid enough to get up a full head of steam in what was always fruitless pursuit often found they could not stop themselves until they reached Aylesbury.

Naphill was a soulless ground surrounded by inter-war housing and the airfields of RAF Bomber Command Headquarters. The terrifying and sudden arrival of a squadron of Harrier jump jets scorching over the sightscreen was certainly responsible for as many wickets as the popgun Naphill attack. M.Bussell hit wicket and shat himself 15 would have been a more accurate reflection of proceedings than the actual entry in the scorebook the first time I played there.

At Pyrton, the fielding side had to contend with a tethered goat that had been given enough rope to be able to encroach the outfield at deep cover point. One year we played Pyrton, the home team were able to run seven while a posse of Radnage fielders tried to retrieve the ball guarded by the stroppy-looking goat. But the batsman paid the price for his opportunism the very next ball. Scarcely able to breathe after the all-run seven he was out bowled to a slow straight one, whereupon he apparently threw up his lunch of four pints, a chilli con carne and a packet of cheese and onion crisps behind the pavilion.

The Radnage wicket was a constant source of complaints from the other clubs in the Mid Bucks League and we were forever being threatened with expulsion if we didn't sort it out. The league had soon realised that their threats to dock us points fell on deaf ears for the simple reason that most seasons we didn't win any points. However, the vexed issue of the wicket was extensively aired at our monthly committee meetings. Held in the old village hall after the over-sixties' beetledrive, the meetings were a cauldron of in-fighting, feuds and rivalries.

Two members of the committee had not been on speaking terms for three years following an unfortunate incident at the annual dinner and dance at Beacon's Bottom Social Club involving the secretary's right hand and the treasurer's wife's left breast. Worse, the second XI captain, Denzil, and Jeff had recently been found scuffling in the pavilion following Denzil's tasteless remarks about Jeff's wife's tasteless sandwiches. Apparently, Denzil had gone into the pavilion kitchen carrying a plate of sandwiches to ascertain the precise nature of the fillings, only to be confronted by Jeff's wife attending to the dirty nappy of one of her enormous brood on the kitchen table. A casual reference to the similarity of the meat paste filling with the contents of her child's nappy provoked a hysterical outburst from Jeff's wife and a flurry of fists from Jeff himself. To the team's ill-concealed delight, Mrs Jeff subsequently withdrew her name from the tea-making rota but the whole episode, rather like her sandwiches, left a nasty taste in the mouth for some months.

Camp David would have been a more appropriate place to hold the meetings, which meant that my instinct for diplomacy and my 'la-di-da way with big words', as they called it, had led to my early appointment to the committee. I was a sort of minister without portfolio whose sole task was to use all my skills of tact when either the subjects of dinner and dances or teas came up on the agenda. Frankly, if by the end of the evening I had managed to keep apart Jeff's fist and Derek's nose, I had done my job.

Rivalry has always been part of the culture of the countryside. Land disputes, access to rivers and streams, grazing rights etc. have pitted village against village for centuries.

Whole villages have been practically at war with each other because of the damming of a stream or a girl getting up the duff by a lad from the rival village. And from the outset, cricket has been seen as a way to express these animosities and tensions without recourse to the pitchfork or four bore. As a newcomer to the village I never really understood why, for instance, Radnagers loathed the good folk from Bledlow Ridge. All I knew is that they did, and that the sentiment was reciprocated.

Perhaps topography has something to do with it. Radnage is located on a ridge of the Chilterns and is accessible by a handful of treacherous twisting hill roads. In bad winters it was quite common for the village to be cut off until the council gritters could get through. Bledlow Ridge in contrast sprawls along the main road of the hill top that hangs above Radnage and from its lofty position offers an unparalleled view of the Chiltern countryside – Buckinghamshire to the east, Oxfordshire to the west. Every day of their lives they looked down on the residents of Radnage and I suppose they felt no reason to do otherwise on the three occasions a year they played us at cricket. Home and away in the league the two teams squared up to each other with points to be won and old scores to be settled, but the mutual contempt was really enshrined in the Ernest Egleton Cup – a once-a-year contest of 40 overs a side on a Sunday which was named after an upwardly mobile native of Radnage who had left the village and walked up the hill to Bledlow.

I suppose I played in four or five of these contests before, during and after my time at university, but the one that sticks out most clearly in my mind is that one in 1980 when tensions between the two teams reached a peak. It was one of those glorious summer's afternoons you only get in H.E.Bates novels: the sun was shining brightly, a distant wood pigeon was providing melodic backing vocals, and mercifully, the wind was not coming from the direction of the pig farm. We had won the toss and decided to bat. Now village cricketers among you will recognise that there are only two things a captain must consider on winning the toss. 1) The quality of the opposition – if they are good, does he want to make sure the game lasts until opening time? If so, bat second. 2) The weather – if it's cold and windy, you bat first. Far better to huddle together in the warmth of the pavilion and send your opening pair out with instructions to build a solid platform for the innings. With a bit of luck, it will rain and you'll never have to risk the frostbite. Similarly, if it's scorching hot, you bat first. Far better to enjoy another beer in the shade of the pavilion and send your openers out with instructions to build a solid platform for the innings. With a bit of luck, it will have cooled down by the time you have to field.

The Radnage innings featured a number of familiar elements. Malcolm was involved in a run out though this time he was the victim of his own suicidal call for a short single:

Malcolm: Yes.
Bob: No!
Malcolm: Come on!
Bob: Get back!
Malcolm: Come on!!!
Bob: Fuck off.
Malcolm: Shit.
Bob: You prat.

Chunky combined stubborn defence with muscular heaves to put together a score that teetered on the brink of 'jug avoidance'. For most of us, passing 50 is a cause for some celebration and to this end the batsman concerned traditionally buys a jug of ale after the match which acts as a soothing balm for the bruised egos of the bowlers. For the tightwads in the team, however, this is a terrifying prospect. Even in 1980 a jug cost the best part of a fiver and some preferred to fall on their sword than risk the financial penalty that went with a half-century. As a deterrent, therefore, the team had introduced a new scheme by which a batsman could still be made to buy a jug if in the opinion of the majority of his teammates he had deliberately got out in sight of his fifty. And as Chunky mowed a full toss straight into mid-on's midriff the jury in the pavilion sat in judgement.

At 140 for four, with 12 overs to go, the stage was set for Ian. If he came off today and hung around for half an hour, we could post a score well out of Bledlow's reach. He walked to the crease. It was the slow walk of a hired gunslinger. His sunhat pulled down over his eyes, a rolled fag spat out on the way to the wicket, a baggy sleeveless jumper that from a distance looked like a poncho, Ian was our Clint Eastwood about to run the bad guys from The Ridge out of town. He held one finger up to the umpire – one leg was his guard. No words were said. No words were needed. We all knew what was about to unfold. Spectators who had seen Ian bat before moved their cars, women grabbed their young children from the boundary's edge and shepherded them to safety. Picture the film of this scene. Sergio Leone is cutting to and from the sweating bowler – beads of sweat forming on his brow – and Ian's grizzled stubbly face. Ennio Morricone's soundtrack is reaching its climax. The bowler starts his run up as the church clock strikes four. He bowls. Ian swings. Ian misses. The bowler hits. First ball again. And as he trudged back to the pavilion you could hear the Monday morning sound of meat cleaver on tenderloin as Ian gave vent to his fury. It was enough to make you turn vegetarian.

Dick then scored his habitual duck and only some clean

hitting from the captain and some timely edges from the tail allowed us to take tea with any degree of comfort. A target of 180 was not by any measure an invincible total, but at village level with this score you won more than you lost.

The Bledlow innings, however, got off to a flier. Our opening bowlers were at their most profligate and some free hitting meant The Ridge had passed 50 before the seventh over was completed. There then followed a sequence of events the like of which I have never seen on a cricket pitch before. First, Dick, squatting bravely at short leg with his hands characteristically fanned out in front of his face in catching mode, was hit full square on the pelvis and had to be carried off. Now, it is not an uncommon occurrence for leg-side fielders in close to be injured. It requires courage and exceptional reflexes to field there and everyone who has spent much time at short leg has the bumps and bruises to show for it. Brian Close was renowned for his foolhardy fielding two yards from the bat and regularly took blows to body and bonce alike in an era before the wearing of helmets was commonplace. Indeed, legend has it that on one occasion the batsman creamed the ball on to Close's nut where it then looped up in the air to be caught by the fielder running in from cover. Close was groggy and bleeding from the head as his teammates, concerned for his well-being, scooped him off the turf.

'Did he catch it?' Close asked as they held smelling salts under his nose.

'Yes, but hell, Brian, what would have happened if it had hit you two inches to the left?' enquired a shell-shocked teammate surveying the large cut just to the side of Close's temple.

'He'd have been caught in t'gully,' came the blunt response.

Doubtless Close was hit more frequently in his long career

than Dick was, but I bet Close was never hit by his own bowler. That was the fate of poor Dick that day. Phil had been spraying it about more than usual but he refused to compromise his speed in striving for greater accuracy and when the footholds gave way in his delivery stride, a wild delivery went winging down the leg side and right into Dick's hip. Dick fell to the ground as if hit by . . . well, a hard sphere of compacted leather at a speed of 50 m.p.h. from 20 yards away and following a brief examination from our wicket-keeping GP he was carried off the field clutching to his side a tea towel full of ice cubes.

We were down to ten men. So Eddie's twelve-year old son, John, who had enjoyed up until then a most pleasant afternoon playing with a frisbee, was press-ganged into service down at fine leg. Here, he did very little except get shouted at with conflicting advice by ten deranged adults on the few ocasions the ball went near him. 'In hard!' 'Bowler's end!' 'Batsman's end!' 'Pick it up!' 'Use your foot!' was the cacophony of instructions John would hear and so it was hardly surprising when he let the first one go straight through his legs for four. 'Head up, John.' 'Don't worry.' 'Next time, nipper.' Cries of sympathy tinged with frustration rang out. It took just two hours of cricket for John to be turned off the game for ever and it was noticeable that he and his frisbee were never seen again near the ground on match days.

The contest was evenly poised at 120 for four when a cover drive sent Graham sprinting to the boundary to save the four. He clawed the ball back just inside the rope but could not stop his own momentum and went careering through the pavilion door followed moments later by a loud crash. The batsmen duly ran three but on investigation in the pavilion Graham was found to have crashed into the bar, taking a table of empty glasses with him and cutting his hand in the process. Blood gushed everywhere from his palm as Eddie's first aid skills with a bottle of TCP and an old hanky were stretched to the limit. A precautionary trip to casualty, however, was called for so we were back down to ten men. And it was here when the tone of the day took a turn for the worse. We asked if we could borrow one of The Ridge's chaps as a substitute fielder but this was met with a point-blank refusal. Now in village cricket substitute fielders on loan from the other side are always something of a lottery. It is taken as read that the fielder offered is always the most inept – unathletic, unlikely to catch it, and with a 'handbag throw'. But what really preys on the mind is the festering conviction that not only is the borrowed fielder naturally inept, but that he is designedly so, too; that were the ball to go to him, he would intentionally drop it. It is a cancer of distrust that quickly spreads through the fielding team. Seething resentments and heated recriminations bubble under the surface and frankly you're often better off with ten men and concentrating on your own game than put up with the half-hearted presence of some flannelled fifth columnist. That said, for our request to be met with such a wanton absence of grace and such a niggardly adherence to the letter of the laws of the game, provoked a marked deterioration in what little goodwill existed between the two teams.

Five overs later, a hot and bothered Jeff raced to the wicket and leapt into his frenetic bowling action only for the ball to bobble accidentally from his grip towards midwicket. In normal circumstances such an incident would have been greeted with a ribald remark or two from various quarters before the ball was declared dead and returned to the bowler to start all over again. On this occasion, however, the batsman advanced from the crease with the intention of scything the now stationary ball to the boundary. Jeff was instantly outraged and bore down on the batsman who in turn sought a ruling from his team's umpire. It was decreed that technically, since the ball had gone forward of the popping crease, the batsman was entitled to a free hit. By now Jeff was fit to burst. He decided that technically he was entitled to field the ball off his own bowling and so he stood with his foot cocked inches over the ball ready to trap it. The batsman sought a further ruling but by now the umpires had lost the stomach for the fight and just shrugged their shoulders. The batsman looked up at Jeff standing defiantly over the ball. All was motionless, everything seemed suspended in time. Then the batsman took a full swing and crunched his bat down on Jeff's ankle. Jeff hopped in agony as the batsman now turned his attention to the ball but before he could lash it for four, Jeff had grabbed him by the throat. They fell to the ground in a whirl of arms and legs, but when the non-striker tried to pull Jeff off his batting partner rather too roughly for our liking a full-scale brawl erupted that took two or three minutes to defuse.

An uneasy truce was finally agreed when the two protagonists were separated and as noses bled and eyes puffed up Jeff limped down to third man. I'd seen John Snow shoulder barge Gavaskar, Javed Miandad and Dennis Lillee scrap fleetingly, and Colin Croft charge into an umpire in New Zealand, but a full-scale rumpus like this was a first. Technically, we now had eight and a half men plus a reluctant twelve-year-old. Dick limped back on the field but was even less capable of running than normal and the game progressed thereafter in a subdued atmosphere. The Bledlow batting fell away in the lower order and Radnage finally wrested the Egleton Cup from The Ridge's grasp when their number 11 holed out to Dick at mid-on with a thumping flat-bat pull. It was just as well he caught it. If he hadn't, he'd have been getting his jaw fixed at the same time as his pelvis.

We drove back to The Crown in Radnage and triumphantly placed the cup on the mantelpiece. But there was an uneasy feeling. We had won but it was victory tinged with regret that we had made our own considerable contribution to the debasing of the noble game of village cricket.

CHAPTER FIVE

There's Only One Perry Digweed
A sorry life as a Surrey fan

Essex v Surrey

Date: 28–31 May 1983   *Venue:* Chelmsford

Essex

G.A.Gooch	b Thomas	1
B.R.Hardie	b Clarke	16
*K.W.R.Fletcher	c Lynch b Monkhouse	10
K.S.McEwan	c Lynch b Knight	45
K.R.Pont	b Pocock	12
N.Phillip	b Pocock	8
S.Turner	c and b Knight	20
R.E.East	c Lynch b Clarke	19
†D.E.East	c Butcher b Pocock	17
N.A.Foster	not out	19
D.L.Acfield	run out	0
Extras	(B4, LB10, NB6)	20
Total		287

Bowling	O	M	R	W
Clarke	20	3	58	2
Thomas	20	2	78	1
Monkhouse	13	2	49	1
Knight	17	6	33	2
Pocock	19.5	6	49	3

Surrey

A.R.Butcher	c D.E.East b Phillip	2	c Gooch b Foster	5
G.S.Clinton	c D.E.East b Foster	6	not out	61
A.Needham	b Foster	0	lbw b Phillip	4
*R.D.V.Knight	lbw b Phillip	0	not out	101
M.A.Lynch	lbw b Phillip	0		
†C.J.Richards	c Turner b Phillip	0		
D.J.Thomas	lbw b Foster	0		
I.R.Payne	b Phillip	0		
G.Monkhouse	lbw b Phillip	2		
S.T.Clarke	b Foster	4		
P.I.Pocock	not out	0		
Extras		0	(B1, LB8, W2, NB3)	14
Total		14	(2 wickets)	185

Bowling	O	M	R	W	O	M	R	W
Phillip	7.3	4	4	6	13	2	39	1
Foster	7	3	10	4	13	2	33	1
Turner					7	3	16	0
Gooch					22	6	45	0
Acfield					17	7	23	0
R.E.East					1	0	5	0
Pont					5	1	10	0

Some years ago, I accompanied a friend of mine who is a Brighton supporter to the Goldstone Ground. It was a grim 0–0 draw on a wet Wednesday but a visit made worthwhile because of one of the most absurd supporters' chants I have ever heard. Following a reflex save mid-way through the second half by the Brighton goalkeeper, the Seagulls supporters decided to show their appreciation by chanting: 'There's only one Perry Digweed.' This went on for the best part of a minute and not once was there the remotest hint of irony in their voices despite the long odds against there being two Perry Digweeds in this solar system, let alone this world. It encapsulated for me the madness that is in every fan for here was a chant full of devotion from people blind to the wider lunacy of what was being said.

But let me spool back further to 1973, with Dad and me sitting in what is now known as the Laker stand. Robin Jackman started his long, rather mincing run, bowled an away-swinger on a nagging length that took the edge of Sadiq Mohammed's bat and was snaffled eagerly by Arnold Long behind the wicket. The twenty or so people around us murmured their approval and something less than a ripple of applause broke out to signify the collective joy at this event. Scarcely a moment to resonate in history but it did mark my birth as a Surrey supporter. Until then, I had merely been a lover of cricket unburdened by parochial loyalties, but from that day in May 1973 it was determined that much of my future enjoyment of the sport would be projected through the prism of Surrey County Cricket Club.

Looking back it could have been any number of clubs on whom I could have chosen to lavish my affections. Living as I did in Buckinghamshire, there was no obvious geographical tie I could call upon so some other impetus, some other means of seduction, was going to be required. The first name in my boyhood scorebook is that of M.E.C.J. Norman, an opening bat for Leicestershire of little note other than his excess of christian names. But Mickey and Leicestershire obviously didn't do the trick, nor indeed was it to be their opponents Nottinghamshire in that first televised match I scored. It wasn't to be Warwickshire either, who, with their array of batting talent – Amiss, Kanhai, Jameson, Kallicharran, Murray – were about to be crowned county champions; nor was it Sussex for whom Tony Greig, the then Golden Boy of English cricket, played. No, it was to be Surrey and its players with whom I had just shared this small moment of triumph – the dismissal of Sadiq Mohammed.

It is the act of witnessing that is all-important to the fan – the being there. Those people that keep track of their team's scores only through the papers or on Ceefax are merely 'followers'. But those who make the trek down to the ground with the thermos and tupperware, they are *supporters* and I wanted to, needed to, be a supporter. I wanted the responsibility and with it the joy, the heartbreak, and the despair that is the lot of all supporters. This had to be an all-consuming passion, a full-blown love affair of the champagne, roses and chocolates variety, not a quick leg-over in your lunch hour at a Holiday Inn. Such intensity only comes from being there watching the drama unfold in the here and now. So when Dad and I went to watch that Surrey v Gloucestershire match at The Oval, the die was cast.

I had been a genuine football fan for a whole year previously – Dad had taken me to see Tottenham v Leicester City (1–0, Martin Chivers) – so I thought I knew what was expected of me, but it was all vastly different to the raucous occasion at White Hart Lane. There I had heard the tribal chanting, seen the fighting, and inhaled the hatred. Here, at The Oval, then as now, I heard the snoring, saw the sharing of sandwiches, and inhaled the pipe tobacco. It was clear to me even then how very different in make-up are football fans from their cricketing equivalents. Football fans were boisterous and confrontational; cricket fans were meek and mild. Football fans were young working-class lads full of pent-up aggression; cricket fans were elderly middle-class coves full of Earl Grey tea. Football fans would jump up and down, spit, and urinate in people's pockets; cricket fans would doze off, dribble, and urinate in their own pockets. But the strength of affection and loyalty, the deep-rooted desire to be there in the thick of it, is present in both groups. It is just expressed differently. I too am much more restrained at a cricket match, my feelings more internalised but the range of emotions are no different, the belief that my presence at the ground is crucial to the prospects of my team is not diminished one jot. This is probably the central psychosis in every sports fan.

You see every true fan has convinced himself that his team actually needs him – it needs his concern, the positive energy that he emits when at the ground. Now some sceptics might think this absolute twaddle, but I can confirm its veracity. In fact I have proven it scientifically under laboratory conditions at The Oval. The match was Surrey v Worcestershire in 1994, the semi-final of the NatWest Trophy. Worcestershire batted first and, courtesy of two hundreds from Moody and Curtis and some lamentable Surrey bowling, scored a mammoth 357 for two in the 60 overs (Curtis 136n.o., Moody 180n.o.). Surrey were in a fix. If we were going to win this it needed some pretty extraordinary performances both on and off the field. The Surrey batsmen had to do their stuff and I had to do mine.

I got to work. Positive vibes flowed from me. Love rays homed in on the Surrey batsmen. Nobody quite stayed in long enough to play the innings that counted but everyone chipped in – Bicknell 89, Thorpe 49, Brown 52 and Hollioake 60 off 36 balls. As dusk fell Surrey needed an improbable 19 off the last over with Joey Benjamin, our number 10, facing. Benjamin nailed two sixes off Lampitt's first four balls and we were left with seven required from the final two balls. Could Joey hit another one? The excitement was intense but I could bear the strain no more. As Lampitt trudged in to bowl the penultimate ball, I hid my head in my hands. Surrey had done this to me too often. In 25 years of supporting them, I had one Benson and Hedges Cup in 1975 and one NatWest Trophy in 1982 to show for it. This paltry return was from a team that had won the championship more times than anyone bar Yorkshire and in the fifties had dominated English cricket with seven straight championships. This was the club of Laker and Lock, the Bedser twins, Barrington and May, Loader and Edrich let alone Hobbs and Sandham, and now we struggled to beat the likes of Leatherdale and Lampitt in the Worcestershire line-up.

A collective gasp could be heard as Joey smote high, wide and handsome towards the Vauxhall End. Airborne, or so I'm told, it looked a six all over. But then Tom Moody, all 9ft 6in of Australian bastard, loomed from out under the shadow of the stand. He leapt, threw up an unfeasibly long limb and caught the sodding thing. Worcestershire had won and it was all my fault. If I'd been watching and willing, Moody wouldn't have got near it. Just when the boys really needed me, I had failed them.

Now there are others who believe the opposite – that no matter how hard we try to send positive vibes, they are perversely converted into negative ones. In fact these poor wretches believe that their mere attendance at a match has a seriously detrimental effect on the team. The really paranoid among this group actually believe *they* are the reason for the team's failure.

Kierkegaard understood this state of mind only too well. Now Kierkegaard is a name that doesn't regularly crop up in cricket books. I have combed *Wisden* in search of an entry along the lines of: S. Kierkegaard (Copenhagen University and Denmark), RHB, OB. HS 45* v The Existentialists at Paris 1896, etc. but to no avail. Yet here is a man who intuitively understood what it is like being a cricket fan. In his essay 'The Unhappiest Man', Kierkegaard defines the state of unhappiness as an inability to enjoy the present and instead a willingness to live only in the past or the future. The unhappy man is always either remembering or hoping. Either he thinks things were better in the past or he hopes they'll be better in the future, but they are always bad *now*. So watching one of Surrey's woefully inept spinners of recent vintage, James Boiling or Chris Bullen say, toiling away for over after over without extracting any discernible turn, I might find myself thinking wistfully of Pat Pocock or hoping against hope that young Richard Pearson might turn into a modern-day Jim Laker. That is apparently run-of-the-mill unhappiness, but the unhappiest man of all is what Kierkegaard calls the 'unhappy hoper', a man who finds gratification in disappointment. This is the state of mind I and countless other fellow supporters find ourselves in throughout the summer. At the onset of every match, I hope Surrey will win but if they do I often hardly notice because I have made myself so miserable imagining how they will lose; and if they *do* lose, this only confirms my underlying belief that they would do so all along and that is somehow gratifying.

Two matches in 1996 seemingly illustrate Kierkegaard's paradigm perfectly. The penultimate game in the AXA Equity and Law Sunday League was played against fellow title contenders Northants at The Oval. Following a century from David Capel, Surrey were set 235 to win and soon lost the cream of their batting in Bicknell, Stewart, Thorpe and Hollioake for well under 100. Surrey needed to win this game to go into the final round of matches level on points with Notts, who had an inferior scoring rate, and to put clear water between us and Northants in third place. The way things were going I was already accepting defeat. Ally Brown hit a typically whirlwind 50 before falling victim to a highly dubious decision from umpire (and Surrey old boy) Trevor Jesty. Five wickets down and not even half way, Nadeem Shahid and the mercurial Chris Lewis sliced, carved and drove their way to 159 before Shahid was trapped in front by Emburey. But Lewis with help first from Brendon Julian (16), and then Martin Bicknell (19), got us to within sight of an unlikely victory until he holed out to extra cover in the final over with us needing just four to win. 'Typical of Lewis,' I muttered miserably. I'd long felt that if you wanted to see a 'choker' in sport, you need look no further than the great shiny-headed one. In came Pearson and there was much playing and missing in the gloaming before a scrambled two left us requiring just two measly runs for victory off the last ball. Bailey, the Northants skipper, juggled his fielders, desperate to stop two runs being taken in the great expanse of The Oval outfield when

Kevin Curran came in to bowl the final delivery. I stared blankly into the gloom awaiting disaster when Bicknell thrashed the ball for four through straight mid-wicket. The sizeable crowd erupted and spilled on to the pitch to embrace the cavorting batsmen who in turn sprinted, bats aloft, for the safety of the pavilion. A variation of Skinner and Baddiel's football anthem from Euro 96 broke out as Surrey supporters sang 'Cricket's coming home' but I sat in my seat numb to victory, scarcely able to comprehend it, so well had I convinced myself of impending failure. Triumph, as was so often the case, passed me by. My conditioned disposition was despair following close defeat. That was what I was used to. I could prepare myself for that as I had done just a few weeks earlier at The Oval for the semi-finals of the NatWest Trophy against Essex.

To the neutral observer 260, courtesy of a fine century from Alec Stewart, was a useful, if not an imposing, total on a good wicket against a strong batting side (Gooch, Law, Hussein, Irani), but certainly a score that gave your bowlers something to defend. But not for the unhappy hoper already drowning his sorrows in Foster's in the Bedser Stand and warning all those around him that 'We're thirty to forty runs short on this wicket'. The early wickets of Grayson and Hussein were a false dawn. The initially limpet-like Gooch came out of his shell (if that's what limpets come out of) and the Australian, Stuart Law, flailed the Surrey bowling to all parts saving the best of his savage hitting for his fellow countryman, Brendon Julian. This blitz gave Essex the upper hand and though wickets fell later – at 210 for six Surrey had a faint whiff of victory, if they could dismiss Irani and wicket-keeper Rollins cheaply – the Essex boys ultimately prevailed with overs to spare. We had lost and I had been right that we would lose, and bizarrely found this disappointment quite gratifying until it occurred to me in a sudden shaft of light: what a thoroughly silly way of spending a life – getting pleasure out of the very things you don't want to happen. But that, as they say, is cricket (at least if you're a Surrey fan).

It poses another philosophical question, though, all this. Am I an unhappy hoper who happens to be a Surrey fan? Or, am I an unhappy hoper *because* I am a Surrey fan? Well, old Soren certainly felt that the extent of our ability to experience pleasure was directly linked to the extent of our previous suffering, which would certainly explain my hysterical behaviour at the sight of Alec Stewart lifting the silverware (or perspexware in the case of the AXA Equity and Law Trophy) on that heady September's afternoon in Cardiff in 1996 when we brought to a close fourteen barren years by winning the Sunday League. It's strange that Denmark, a country whose sole contribution to the pageant of cricket history has been the Derbyshire trundler, Ole 'Stan' Mortensen, should produce a man in Soren Kierkegaard who so understands cricket and the associated suffering, but I would respectfully suggest to all Durham supporters that he become required reading as a matter of urgency.

Certainly Monday 30 May 1983 was a day to go scuttling off with a tome of Kierkegaard, a bottle of Thunderbird pear wine, and a packet of Prozac. Surrey had been playing cricket for 119 years since they had won the inaugural championship in 1864, but chose my first visit to Chelmsford to record their lowest total ever. In just 14 overs we were skittled for 14 runs – five wickets falling while the score was on 8 and only an agricultural swipe for four from Sylvester Clarke saved us from the ignominy of scoring the lowest first-class score ever. These were the dark days of Surrey cricket – Clinton, Needham, Thomas, Payne and

Monkhouse were never likely to enter the Surrey pantheon, while Lynch, Richards and Clarke were touched with a very erratic genius. This was a team whose collective digit, along with that of its supporters, was forever hovering over the self-destruct button.

Now, the 'County of the White Sock' is never a nice place to have your nose rubbed in it. There's an impregnable cockiness to the Essex teams which is matched by their supporters, and watching Norbert Philip making mincemeat of your middle-order surrounded by the braying denizens of Brentwood and Billericay is hard to stomach. Essex are newcomers to the top table of English cricket, but since their Benson and Hedges Cup win in 1979, their first-ever trophy, they have been conspicuous by their success and a whole generation of Essex supporters has grown up knowing nothing else. It seems pathetic to be seething with anger at other people merely because they are happy, but that's how I felt about those Essex supporters as they pranced deliriously around me with the fall of every wicket. I loathed their smug little faces and their smug little laughs as the Surrey scorecard took on the look of some binary calculation. Essex were destined to win the championship again that year but did they have to flaunt their success so insensitively? Did they have any idea what it was like watching Grahame Clinton bat? Or Giles Cheatle bowl? Or David 'Teddy' Thomas fall over? (The poor lad had developed an unfortunate tendency to hurl himself to the ground at the moment of delivery and it was often a close-run thing whether he bounced off the pitch higher than the ball.)

Essex are not the worst offenders though. That honour is won hands down by Lancashire. When the Red Rose comes down to London, it brings with it all the chippy Mancunian resentment of being the country's second city and when Lancashire play at The Oval, it seems they're not just taking on Surrey but the whole Establishment and the London conspiracy to do Manchester down. In the sixties it was Liverpool that set itself up in opposition to London. Now, with its successful cultural icons of Oasis, Manchester United, Mrs Merton *et al.*, the constant chorus of 'Ooh Lanky, Lanky!' is tinged with a more abrasive edge. Yorkshire, too, has a vocal and cocksure support borne of its historical record as the game's most successful club and a generation of cricketers – Trueman, Close, Boycott and Illingworth – whose legendary cussedness and conceit still strike a chord with the supporters. I have never believed the saying 'When Yorkshire is strong, England is strong', but what is undoubtedly true is that when Yorkshire is strong, its supporters are even more of a pain in the arse than usual.

These passions for sports teams are tribal in their origins. It goes much deeper than a whimsical preference for one set of players. The true fan embraces the folklore of the club, its heritage, its playing traditions, its whole culture to the point where it is in some way an expression of the man himself. So when others laugh at your team, they laugh at you.

This wasn't tolerated in football, at least not in the hooligan days of old. If the opposing fans got up your nose, they soon got a Doc Marten up theirs. And for a few brief moments as I watched this abject humiliation, I lost my *Guardian* reader principles of social responsibility and fantasised about a Surrey fan's response to this Essex crowing football-style. I had visions of me and the other five or so travelling Surrey fans kicking over a bench and 'taking the Chelmsford pavilion' in the way Spurs fans tried every year 'to take the Clock End' at Arsenal. But my fellow Surrey fans scarcely looked like the cricketing equivalent of the Inter City Firm. The ICF, you will recall, was a cabal of West Ham supporters who took the gangland ethics of the East End to the terraces. Members of the ICF would ride the Football Specials – filthy trains put on by British Rail to transport fans the length and breadth of the country – terrorising all and sundry. They would carry with them knuckledusters, Stanley knives and razor blades, and famously would leave a calling card on their bruised and bleeding victims that read 'You have been visited by the Inter City Firm.' But my fellow Surrey fans, the nylon nerds at Chelmsford that day, were more likely to be carrying bicycle clips than bicycle chains. I would just have to grin and bear it.

It was certainly the nadir of 25 years of service to the club. When I was baptised and joined The Oval congregation in 1973, Surrey were still a force to be reckoned with. They had won the championship under Micky Stewart in 1971, Edrich and Arnold were stalwarts of the current England team, Roope and Pocock were on the fringe, and we had the Young Cricketer of the Year in Dudley Owen-Thomas (one of the least prescient bits of judging from any panel ever!) Things were looking bright, so much so that we could not find a regular place for the young Bob Willis in the side. But it was an efficient utilitarian outfit rather than one blessed with flair. Even our overseas players lacked sparkle and a consistent match-winning ability. Hampshire had Greenidge and Barry Richards, Lancashire had Clive Lloyd, Notts had Sobers, Essex had Keith Boyce. We relied on the more prosaic services of Younis Ahmed and Intikhab Alam and this disparity of effectiveness inculcated in me a dread and loathing of star players that I still have. It is marked too by being in direct proportion to the player concerned. The better they are, the more I can't bear them.

As genuine supporters rather than followers, we do not go to matches to watch a Viv Richards masterclass or a Mark Waugh command performance. We go to watch them get nought, hopefully, and Jason Ratcliffe (or whoever) grind out a century. That's our idea of a good day's cricket, not

Carl Hooper strutting his stuff. (Unless of course you are a fan of Kent, or even I suppose a Kentish fan.) Only the neutral likes the unpredictable genius of the overseas player. But there are those occasions when the visiting star does fail and a non-star plays out of his skin. If you are at the receiving end of this, it can be even worse.

The year 1994 was indisputably Brian Lara's and when Warwickshire came to Guildford, Charles, a barrister friend of mine, asked if he could come along in the hope of seeing a Lara special. I looked at him with ill-concealed contempt. Surrey and Warwickshire were running neck-and-neck for the championship (Surrey having won five out of their first seven championship matches) and the last thing we needed was that little sod running riot, I thought. But I acquiesced. Charles is a good companion at such occasions and a willing runner to and from the beer tent.

We arrived late thanks to an epidemic of traffic cones on the A3 but in time to see Lara caught by Thorpe off Cameron Cuffy for 2. Charles was devastated; the *raison d'être* of his day snuffed out so early. I was ecstatic and more so as I watched Brummie batters troop in and out in quick succession. But Surrey's fortunes nosedived with a triple whammy from four Warwickshire nonentities which made for some of the most grim spectating in recent memory.

First, Welch and the debutant, Brown, put on 110 precious first-innings runs for the ninth wicket, then Roger Twose with his bustling 'dobblers' took six for 28, before the tubby Andy Moles trudged his way to what is, according to *Wisden*, 'the slowest double century in championship history'. Now I can't bear cruelty to animals any more than the next man, but what's a bit of lipstick on a bunny rabbit or twenty filter tips a day for a beagle compared to an Andy Moles double hundred? I hatched a plan with Charles, as we drove home enjoying the view of the traffic cones from the other side, that we should set up an organisation to counter such gratuitous cricketing cruelty. Called the Spectators Liberation Front, the organisation's main mission would be to don balaclavas and kidnap the likes of Moles and Twose, thus liberating defenceless spectators from the barbarity of their performances. It came to nothing, of course. For a start, neither of us possessed a balaclava. So Moles is still around the county circuit inflicting misery on good, honest spectators, as indeed are his chums Welch and Brown. Only Twose has shown any public spiritedness by doing the next best thing to the creation of the SLF and going off to play in New Zealand.

But back to that Surrey team of the seventies. Bland it may have been, but it was reasonably competitive, finishing second in the championship in 1973 behind Richard Gilliat's Hampshire all-stars. It was an ageing team, however, and as Edrich, Edwards, Storey, Long and Arnold reached their sell-by dates so performances deteriorated. By the late seventies Surrey's lacklustre playing staff coincided with invigorating performances from teams that had hitherto been seen as championship cannon fodder – Northants, Essex and Somerset, fortified by shrewd overseas signings, all began to assert themselves, particularly in one-day cricket. In contrast, Surrey were a team of bits-and-pieces players that was rarely able to lean on the imported genius of a genuine international star. In 1980 and 1981 we lost finals to Middlesex and Somerset. If we weren't suffocated by the metronomic accuracy of Vincent van der Bijl, we were put to the sword by Viv Richards who hit 132 out of a total of 197. Those bloody international stars again! I was sitting my 'A' levels around this period seeking cogent answers to important academic questions like: Is the novel dead? Or is representative democracy compatible with a culture of tribal autocracy in post-Imperial Africa? But no questions have flummoxed me more, then and now, than why Surrey could never attract players like Richards, Greenidge, Garner, etc. Why did we end up with Geoff Howarth, Younis Ahmed, Dirk Tazelaar and Rudi Bryson? A NatWest Trophy win against Warwickshire which, because of the ridiculous early start in September was all over by lunchtime, was the only highlight for a club that would go on to lose six semi-finals and one final in the next fifteen years, while never quite getting close enough to challenge for the championship. Indeed, it was around the early eighties that my faith began to waver. Maybe cricket was not the centre of the universe. Four years at Southampton University to read politics, philosophy and modern history provided a myriad distractions. More and more I felt able to ignore the peal of bells calling The Oval flock to worship. But did I betray cricket or did cricket betray me? Certainly the team of the mid-eighties was a difficult team to be in love with and in truth it was less the calling of Hegel, Marx and Plato, and much more the incompetence of Pauline, Needham and Monkhouse that weakened my resolve. On my doorstep I could watch Greenidge or Malcolm Marshall in full flow, and later still the emergence of the precocious Robin Smith, and the two-hour drive up the M3 to my beloved Oval was not made any easier by the prospect of seeing the likes of Doughty and Waterman take the new ball. Never heard of them? Precisely.

For the first time in my life cricket and Surrey were relegated way down my list of priorities some way below, and in no particular order, drinking, playing poker, playing pinball and the attractions of Rebecca James' bosom. I left Southampton with a suspect liver, debts that judging from the behaviour of my bank manager were clearly surpassed only by the Brazilian national debt, and a highest score of

4,974,800 at Star Wars Pinball. But it is arguable that I had achieved any less than Surrey.

It was a period of growing unease around the club and tales of unrest in the dressing room. Roger Knight retired and returned to teaching – apparently the prospect of thirty snotty-faced kids was preferable to ten snotty cricketers. Then, first Howarth for two seasons, and Pocock for one, took on the captaincy. Neither, however, shone in this role and in 1987 it was decided by the committee to appoint an outsider untainted by dressing-room rancour and the new broom was to be Ian Greig. I think it was Sam Goldwyn who when asked to summarise the talents of the young Fred Astaire, said something along the lines: 'Balding a little. He can't act, he can't sing, he can dance bit.' Similar thoughts sprang to mind about Ian. He was balding, couldn't bat, couldn't bowl and couldn't field. We were left to hope his dancing would come up to scratch.

Jack Richards, our brilliant but temperamental wicket-keeper, was one of the casualties of the new order with its emphasis on discipline, but the management never properly harnessed the emerging talents of the Bicknell brothers, Stewart, Thorpe and Medlycott, and even when for once Surrey picked an international winner in the shape of Waqar Younis, The Oval remained a trophy-free zone.

One things fans are not is sentimental; 'followers' are. You can still hear 'followers' purring about David Gower, or welling up about Botham in 1981, but the real fan is only interested in tomorrow. Someone might have got a double hundred against Australia in the Test match but if he gets a duck in the following Sunday League game against Glamorgan, he'll still be called a silly sod and criticised for no longer doing it for his county. Such is the fan's fickle attitude to the players. I gave up on Monte Lynch and his eccentric batting long before his departure to Gloucestershire, as I had done with Dudley Owen-Thomas in the early seventies. And when that love is lost, it's hard to win it back. Love and hate are not just convenient four-letter bedfellows when it comes to tattooing your knuckles, they are emotions often separated by a wafer-thin dividing line and it is the players who are the objects of these intense feelings.

Take Chris Lewis: a man with sublime talents but a frustrating tendency not to use them. One day he gets a duck and bowls liquorice allsorts, and I have the wax effigy and drawing pins out, the next day he scores a whirlwind ton and I'd willingly bear his children. Or look at the case of Keith Medlycott: in 1990 he received the ultimate accolade in his sport and got picked for England's tour of the West Indies. He had averaged well over 60 wickets a season for the last three years and as a lower middle-order batsman had a career average just shy of 30, but two years after touring the Caribbean with England and reaching the pinnacle of his profession, he was suddenly unable to get into the Surrey side. He didn't play in 1992 at all. The yips, the heebie-jeebies, call it what you will but Medders had 'lost it'. He could apparently bowl whole overs in the nets unable to make it pitch, or would bowl so short that it would reach the batsman on the second bounce. In sporting terms, it was a human tragedy but within three weeks of the start of the 1992 season most Surrey supporters had forgotten him. Neil Kendrick was the slow left-armer in the Surrey side now and we were putting all our energies and efforts into willing him success. That's the level of sentiment that pervades the hardcore supporter.

It's a single-minded and self-centred devotion too. When Alec Stewart held aloft the giant paperweight otherwise known as the AXA Equity and Law Trophy on the pavilion balcony at Sophia Gardens, I was not particularly pleased for Alec Stewart, as everyone exhorted me to be. I was pleased for myself! Bloody hell! He hadn't had to watch it day in day out for fourteen thankless years. He was forever off gallivanting round the world with the Test team. It was me putting the hours in at home watching Rehan Alikhan move from 9 to 16 in a morning session. No, that bauble was a reward for all those wet Wednesdays in Ilkeston, the débâcle at Chelmsford, the horrible Wasim Akram-induced collapse against Lancashire in the Benson and Hedges Cup. I had earned that crummy thing. Current players like Ben Hollioake weren't even born when I was suffering the slings and arrows of Roy Baker and Andy Mack. After that, winning was never going to be a vicarious pleasure, it was going to be all mine.

It's frightening too the deals you're prepared to make with the Almighty in an attempt to secure victory for your team. Frequently, when the game situation is tense, I find myself bleating to a divine force I don't even believe in, trying to strike a bargain: 'Please let Surrey win. I'll visit Auntie Maud every Sunday if you do.' These prayers are seldom answered and so I seldom drop in on old Maud but if she knew the conditions under which my few brief visits were made – the success of Surrey County Cricket Club – she'd have written me out of the will long ago. The Sunday after our party in Cardiff, I decided to pay Maud a visit. I hadn't been for months, which filled me with guilt, but I also couldn't expunge from my mind a notion that the only reason we had won the Sunday League at all was that the Almighty had belatedly taken me up on one of my earlier offers. I felt sort of cosmically indebted. But when I got to her house unannounced I found Maud and her commode being wedged into the back of a Montego by a man called Clive. It became apparent that Clive and his family (Angela and their two children, Damian and Aisha) had befriended Maud and regularly took her for a drive at weekends. Maud said they had been to Kew Gardens, Richmond Park and Marble Hill in the last month but she couldn't stop because they were off to Streatham Bowl. With that Clive drove off with Maud waving to me through the back window and me dealing with the image of an incontinent old lady let loose on a tenpin bowling alley. What a nice bloke this Clive was, I thought to myself, giving up his Sunday afternoons to take a neighbour for a day out. But then again, he could have been a Warwickshire supporter with a few debts to pay. I thought I had detected a Brummie drone to his voice.

I suppose I could always bring Maud to a Sunday League game at The Oval and kill two birds with one stone. I'm not sure what she would make of the old place. To the outsider it is forbidding and unwelcoming, surrounded as it is by those dreary inter-war council flats and in the shadow of the gasometers. Beyond the Vauxhall End stands the new MI6 building made of yellow and green concrete blocks – a sort of Legoland for spies. At the Pavilion End, the pavilion has been raised to bridge the Bedser Stand with the Laker and Lock stands to form one half of an amphitheatre. Architecturally, it is a mess but the viewing is unsurpassed throughout the country. Nine-tenths empty as it invariably is, the ground looks stark and inhospitable but after 25 years I have grown to love its anonymous torpid atmosphere. It's a wonderful place to be alone and in moments of existential angst I sometimes think how nice it would be to end up here – my ashes scattered on the square – when stumps are drawn for the last time. I quite like the idea of being scattered on a spinner's length making life difficult for opposing batsmen. But then my mate Dave told me about the experience he had had with his Grandfather Jack, a lifelong cricketing fanatic, whose dying wish was for his ashes to be scattered on the cricket pitch of his old prep school. Official requests were made and the school obliged. A date was fixed in March. Dave accompanied his tearful grandmother to the scene of some of Jack's greatest sporting triumphs and they took some time to reflect on how important this place had been to him, how happy his time there had been. Then they opened the plastic urn, to find that owing to the recent damp weather Jack, who had for some months been nestling between the Domestos and the Mr Muscle in the cupboard under the sink, had congealed somewhat into a lumpy mixture that clung to the sides of the plastic tub. Dave did his best to shake and bang the tub in a dignified way, but while the odd speck or two fell to the soil, Jack was clearly having second thoughts. With every thump of the urn Dave's grandmother got more distressed and so with her sobbing copiously into her hanky and the crisp March morning getting colder by the minute, Dave decided drastic measures were required. He determined to give the urn one good violent jerk. As he did, a sudden gust of wind got up and in an instant Jack was blown all over his grandson.

It was some weeks later that I heard this story. Dave was round at the flat indulging in his favourite pastime of drinking my wine, when I noticed that every time he got up from the sofa, he left a grey powdery deposit which on closer inspection and analysis we deduced to be Dave's grandfather. The man was everywhere: in Dave's pockets, in his trouser turn-ups, in his flies. And it occurred to me that this was hardly a fitting final resting place for a cricket fan – down the back of someone's sofa with just two biros, a half-eaten packet of mints, and a 5 drachma coin for company. Not even a Surrey fan deserved that.

CHAPTER SIX

College Daze
University cricket and
touring abroad

C.C. A.K. Amsterdam v Southampton University

Date: 12 August 1984   *Venue:* Amsterdam   *Toss*: Amsterdam

Southampton University

A.Barnes	c Joop b Schubye	31
J.Prentice	lbw b Blair	7
J.Sbresni	b Blair	4
R.Hunter	b Bochove	16
M.Logsdon	c Van Oos b Bochove	12
* I.Geddes	c Romer b Bochove	28
M.Bussell	not out	19
G.Tait	run out	8
† P.Whyte	run out	6
R.Lythgoe	did not bat	
G.Pilcher	did not bat	
Extras		11
Total (8 wickets)		143

Bowling	O	M	R	W
Blair	4	3	4	2
Schubye	12	1	25	1
Bochove	10	3	26	3
Joop	8	1	41	0
Romer	6	1	36	0

C.C. A.K. Amsterdam

J.van Oos	c Whyte b Geddes	12
P.de Ende	b Lythgoe	29
R.Gomes	not out	64
B.Blair	not out	37
Extras		4
Total (2 wickets)		146

Bowling	O	M	R	W
Geddes	6	0	32	1
Lythgoe	5	0	34	1
Pilcher	7	0	41	0
Tait	4	0	18	0
Bussell	3	0	17	0

It's probably not an exaggeration that in the public's hierarchy of demonology students fit in somewhere between Jehovah's Witnesses and traffic wardens. The public has little understanding of what they do, but the general consensus seems to be that they certainly don't do much studying since they are too busy sitting in their duffle coats blocking the pavement outside Tandy as they demonstrate against the imperialist occupation of Baluchistan, or dressing up in women's clothing and pushing hospital beds down the High Street apparently in the name of Third World charity. And if they're not doing that, they are the oiks who leave the pub at closing time, urinate their names in the snow and steal traffic cones.

Even people like me who were fortunate enough to go to university have to fight in later life against these feelings of contempt for students. I live in Clapham, south London, two doors down from a student house. There are now eight of them in a four-bedroom house with the two reception rooms downstairs converted into makeshift bedrooms. They keep themselves pretty much to themselves but they still irritate me.

It is 3.20 a.m. I am lying awake in bed because their front door has just banged for the umpteenth time. Now I can hear the distant but naggingly audible clink, clink, chink of their music. Tomorrow morning (Saturday) the guys will try to patch up their beaten up old Minis and Volkswagens making the street look like it's hosting a spare

123

parts fair. If it's hot tomorrow like it is tonight we will have to put up with the thin girl's endless lovemaking in the back bedroom with the window open. At least I presume that's what it is. Either that or she is a chronic asthmatic. We and the other thirtysomething couples who live nearby will cast disapproving looks at the window whence the wheezing and groaning emanates and huffily turn the sausages on our barbecues. For God's sake. Sex in the afternoon. When will they grow up? But that is the very point. My hatred of students is actually a form of self-hatred. I resent the loss of what I had. It is a hatred born of envy. God, when was the last time I could stay out every night getting pissed down the pub? When was the last time I had sex in the afternoon? That time at my mother's house when she looked after the kids in the garden, and then suddenly burst into the bedroom for a nappy and we had to pretend we were looking for Fran's earring. Yes. Naked. Well, it was the best I could come up with on the spur of the moment. Anyway, the point is I should be more tolerant of students. Hell, it was only fourteen years ago I was a student myself. I was exactly the same. But there again, if that door slams again tonight, I'll shove his traffic cone up his arse!

I had little idea what student life had in store for me when I went down to Southampton. I had been to one of their open days and met some of the teaching staff and undergraduates in the History department, but I had eschewed the tour round the library and the university campus in favour of an afternoon down the County Ground watching Hampshire v Australia. An uninspiring afternoon the highlight of which was a belligerent 72 from Rod Marsh as Steve Malone and John Southern reduced the Aussies to 126 for six.

My parents drove me down with a suitcase of clothes, boxes of books about Socrates, Rousseau and comparative systems of government (the spines of which to this day remain unbroken), that poster of the girl tennis player scratching her bum that every eighteen-year-old male has owned at some point in his life, and a few little extras that Mum had thought of, like coffee mugs, a plate, cutlery and this very snazzy kitchen tool that was an all-in-one tin opener, knife, dicer, potato peeler. It never got used for any cooking as such, but it came in jolly handy for removing the lids from pot noodles which were, as now probably, the staple diet for most students.

I unpacked this assorted junk into my college room-cum-cell as Dad ogled the fresh-faced girls in the quadrangle carrying all kinds of home comforts – hi-fi systems, Persian rugs, microwave ovens, mini fridges – into their rooms. One of the inalienable differences between men and women revealed itself to me that day. Women do not believe in travelling light. Give a man a hi-fi, a TV with Fastext and a poster of a girl tennis player scratching her bum and that's home. No need for all those frills like candles, pictures, bed sheets, or curtains. But this is for another time. Back to my room in Southampton where Mum was explaining to me the first signs of scurvy. There was an awkward pause. I wanted them to go. But Mum needed some gesture of affection between us to punctuate this landmark, the final severing of the apron strings. Dad and I, however, had been in this film many times before. He knew his job was to step on the gas and get the hell out of there before I was caught by someone trying to unclamp Mum's lips from my cheek. Dad shook me by the hand and muttered those things dads say when they don't know what to say. I pre-empted my mother's lunge and gave her a quick peck on the cheek and they left. I watched them walk across the quadrangle, passing a father carrying a two-seater sofa into the women's block, and then they slipped out of view.

I turned and surveyed my spartan room, the inventory for which ran as follows: one bed (purposely narrow to discourage nocturnal visitors), one desk, one desk chair, one easy chair, one shelf, one wardrobe (door missing), and one rug (4ft x 3ft) that lay on a wooden floor. This rug I later came to learn was ingeniously designed to collect all the dirt and fluff in the room and then allow easy transfer of said dirt and fluff into bed via feet. I blue-tacked up my tennis girl poster and fiddled distractedly with the kitchen tool. For a moment or two I was overcome with a sense of melancholy – what was I doing in this dump? What the hell did I want with lectures on Plato, Descartes and the Ghanaian civil service? But before I could spiral too far into depression my eyes fell on the yellow dust jacket of the 1981 *Wisden*. I picked it out of the box and turned randomly to a page containing the scorecard of the first Test against West Indies at Nottingham – a Test match that West Indies won by just two wickets but only after some desperate slogging from Andy Roberts when England had reduced them to 180 for seven chasing 208 to win. Before I knew it, I was floating away in a warm mist of memories. Cricket had once again shown itself to be my constant companion in my moment of need.

The television adaptation of *Brideshead Revisited* was broadcast just prior to my arrival at Southampton and having no older siblings as appropriate role models it was this and books like *Lucky Jim* that, more than anything, moulded my preconceptions of university. As a result I was expecting a world of intensely intellectual sophisticates wafting about in tweed suits clutching teddy bears to their chests and quaffing vintage port over arguments about the Bauhaus movement. How on earth was an intellectual pygmy like me going to hold his own in the academic hothouse of the junior common room? I need not have worried. On the first night, as I walked across the quadrangle back to my room in Connaught Hall, I witnessed the less than edifying spectacle of five blokes 'mooning' at the blocks housing the female students. On each buttock had been painted a letter and, as they stood in a drunken, raucous line, I could see their arses read: 'WE LOVE YOU!'. Three nights later in the union bar, patrons were treated to an impromptu display of drinking games by the rugby club. This included 'Rectumpence', a jolly little game that involved dropping your trousers, trapping a 50p coin between two clenched cheeks and waddling down the length of the bar before squatting over a pint mug and depositing the coin therein. The climax of the show was an exhibition of 'turtling', so named because when the scrotal sack is pulled back, up and over the hanging member, the overall effect is to make the rearranged genitalia look like a turtle. Next time you consume a litre of cherry brandy you can try it yourself. That first week made it clear that if Sebastian Flyte had gone to Southampton rather than Oxford, he would have spent far less time sipping champagne and worrying about his homosexuality and instead got on with the real fun of being a student – pouring lager over your head while your friends tattoo 'Ooh Aah Cantona' across your backside.

I had no idea it was going to be like this and to be honest it wasn't long before I, too, was entering into the yobbish student spirit, though I never quite got to the point of exposing my bum in public. But in those early days I was very much in *Lucky Jim* mode. To my acute embarrassment now, I took to smoking a pipe and wearing a brown corduroy jacket with leather patches on the elbows. I would prop up the hall bar puffing away and drinking real ale, and occasionally thumbing an old copy of Camus' *The Outsider*. I assumed I looked wonderfully eccentric and debonair and that young lovelies would swoon at this vision of suave educated manhood. As it was I looked like the young relief geography master who prefers to hang out with the kids rather than go to the staff room. His mistake is to think they like his self-consciously unstuffy liberal ways when the reality is they think he's a complete berk. It wasn't long before I realised the 'pipe and Tolstoy' image had to go.

It is one of the great virtues of further education, however, that it gives you the time and space to reinvent yourself. You can throw away all the baggage from home and school and start afresh with a new batch of friends. That certainly must have been the thinking of my fellow Old Borlasian 'Melon'. 'Melon' had acquired his nickname after being caught in the boarding house showers at midnight stark naked while holding a melon with a two-inch diameter hole bored into it. Despite his protestations, it was impossible to stop the boys who had discovered him jumping to the obvious conclusions as to the purpose of this piece of fruit. His embarrassing discovery was gleefully broadcast to the entire school the following day and from then on the fruity epithet stuck. It was an incident that plagued him during the rest of his schooldays and it must have been with some relief that he was finally able to escape his past and relaunch himself at university. Imagine, then, the expression on the poor sod's face when I ambled up behind him in the refectory queue, tapped him on the shoulder and boomed: 'Melon! What the hell are you doing here?' He stuttered an explanation of sorts, his eyes all the time imploring me to drop the 'Melon' refrain. I chuntered about nothing in particular as the refectory queue slowly snaked its way to the serving area, but I was conscious of an air of discomfort and the knuckles of his hands holding the tray visibly tensed as the cook enquired whether he wanted trifle or melon. I understood his look of despair –

the look of a man whose hopes of escaping his past were hanging in the balance. His hopes for a new life were in my hands. 'The trifle looks good,' I announced. Tears of joy tinged with relief welled up in his eyes.

During freshers' week I signed up to join the university cricket club and put my name down for the winter nets in the indoor school at the County Ground. Here was my chance to reinvent myself as a cricketer. A couple of decent nets and suddenly I could become a dashing middle-order batsman and handy off-spinner, rather than the stone-walling opener and occasional bowler the school had pigeonholed me as. It took about five balls for everyone to reach the obvious conclusion about my batting prowess when my stumps were clattered for the third time. My forward lunge had let me down badly. I slumped off to the bowling net where I managed to catch the eye of the second XI captain with a few off-breaks and I was pencilled in as a second team squad member. I had come to university as a school first-team regular and had relaunched myself as a peripheral member of the second team.

What I had failed to appreciate, however, was that Southampton University CC was just like any other club I was to play for thereafter. It might have had a pool of fifty potential players, but the reality was the second XI captain normally had only six definites on the Friday evening before the match. Saturday mornings were spent by the captain driving from house to house sobering up the drunk, bribing the reluctant, and dragging the lucky lying in bed out from under their girlfriends and into whites. It was a job that required tact, nurse-maiding, bullying and a ruthless willingness to blackmail (with or without photographs).

The university played in Hampshire's premier club league and the responsibility to field eleven players was felt acutely by the captains. It was the minimum benchmark of competence for a club which for some time had fought a rearguard battle against expulsion from the league, which did not look favourably on the variable standard of teams we put out. If you were unlucky, you could meet a Southampton University team that boasted three county trialists, two former Welsh Schools caps and a Zimbabwe U-19 international. If you were lucky you could play against a team whose members had variously been up all night copulating with nymphomaniacs from the local nursing college, arrived at the ground in black tie direct from an all-night party, got stoned and gone to bed hugging a traffic cone, or (perhaps most memorably) spent the night of their 21st birthday padlocked to a parking meter wearing nothing but their 'Y'-fronts and with the word 'Dick' written on their forehead in lipstick. One week we would trounce the league leaders; the next week we would be bowled out for 35 by one of the strugglers. Our fixtures could be guaranteed to throw up the extraordinary. And unfortunately, during many matches so could our players.

As a second team player, it meant that one week you were playing in closely fought matches against decent club players, and the next week having been drafted into the first team at the last minute you were chasing leather against Trojans CC as a young lad by the name of Robin Smith ran amok or fending away brutishly quick stuff from the likes of Bournemouth's Kevin Emery who in the 1982 county championship had taken 78 wickets at 22.19 in harness with Marshall, before losing his action and reluctantly returning to club cricket.

The highlight of the cricketing calendar was always the Universities Athletic Union tournament which was designed to find the best university team in the country, excluding Oxford and Cambridge. Four zonal matches were played with the top two teams from each group going through to the knockout stage. Durham and Loughborough had traditionally dominated the tournament, Durham winning fourteen times and Loughborough eleven times since the inaugural tournament in 1927. Durham fielded players in the eighties of the calibre of Paul Allott, Graeme Fowler and Nasser Hussain, while Loughborough attracted the sporting cream of the country to its physical education course. During my time there, Southampton could normally be relied upon to make it to the knockout phase but rarely prospered into the later stages. However, one year we made it to the semi-finals beating Reading (twice), Imperial College, Kent, LSE, Surrey and East Anglia before coming up against Loughborough at home.

We had a strong team that year and batted right down the order but suddenly in that fixture it was men against boys. In fact we had lost before a ball was bowled in anger. As we sat on the pavilion balcony breakfasting on lager and doughnuts we watched in awe as our opponents warmed up. The whole concept of warming up was a novel enough one for us, but the callisthenics and tumbling routines going on below us were something else. Flick-flacks were followed by backward somersaults climaxing with forward rolls completed with that faintly camp flourish all gymnasts possess. The only rolls our blokes were accustomed to were filled with cheese and pickle but we comforted ourselves with the thought that cricket was largely a game played in the mind. Mental fortitude would always overcome physical or technical superiority. But when their opening bowler got his third ball to rear wickedly up at our best batsman who nicked it off the shoulder of the bat and was caught one-handed by second slip diving high to his right, what little mental toughness we possessed dribbled away. He was quick that bowler and our waiting batsmen were a sorry sight as they squabbled over the rarely used thigh pads and wedged folded towels down the legs of their trousers. Fortitude of mind is always desirable but in some cases fortitude of bowel is more important.

In 1984 in the summer of my final year at Southampton, the club undertook a ten-day tour of Holland. The squad of fourteen players comprised a mixture of first and second team players and a number of the stereotypes to be found in most teams. Led by Ian, our affable captain with a Corinthian spirit and diplomatic manner, we had the grumpy fast bowler in 'The Druid' who was in the habit of shouting 'Get in the hutch, rabbit!' to dismissed batsmen. Sometimes they would counter with 'Piss off you ugly Welsh twat' or words to that effect, whereupon Ian's unruffled diplomacy would be at a premium. Druid was one of those blokes who thrived on being hated. We were booed off the pitch after one match on this tour when he deliberately bowled four leg-side wides to lose us the match and hence deny their opening batsman on 97 the chance of a hundred. Every person he met was a potential adversary, somebody to upset or provoke into argument. I have no idea what he's doing now but whenever I hear someone complaining loudly in public, I always expect to find Lythgoe pinning some poor shop assistant against the wall.

'Hunts' was the beast in our team. Most teams have one. He is the bloke who delights in disgusting you. The one who eats his verrucas, and anybody else's if the wager is attractive enough, and whose jockstrap contravenes both the Environmental Health Act and the United Nations Resolution on human rights. His partner in crime on this tour was PW our wicket-keeper who had grown Godfrey Evans 'Bugger grips' in tribute to the great man and habitually wore a huge stetson everywhere. A man never to resist a challenge, he was one of those apprehended by the Amsterdam police for trying to fire up an outboard motor in the course of an illicit midnight pleasure cruise up and down the city's canals and his constant request to see Detective Van Der Valk (he of the eponymous TV cop show) had apparently only prolonged his detention by the local constabulary. Loggers was our class batting act who always looked good but forever underachieved. He invariably found some ludicrous way of getting out like stumped off a wide, or run out backing up courtesy of a ricochet off the bowler's boot, or caught at mid-off after the ball had hit a low-flying seagull. G-G-G-G-G-G-G-Gordon was our frontline spinner with a stutter who had all the wristy movements, the contorted arms, and the constant licking of fingers to lead you to expect something more devilish than the lollipops he habitually dispensed. While 'Pouncer', our first-change bowler, made South Africa's Paul Adams (whose action was memorably described as resembling a frog caught in a blender) look positively orthodox.

That said, we were confident we had enough collective talent to deal with anything these Dutch clubs could throw at us. After all, we were English. We had invented the damn game. It was in our blood; part of our national heritage. Cricket in Holland was merely the domain of a few Anglophile eccentrics. But we were in for a shock. Our record at the tour's end was: Played 8, Won 1, Drawn 1, Lost 6. It was a record that seemed to impugn our very Englishness. How could eleven Englishmen lose to eleven Dutchmen at cricket – that most quintessentially English of games? Football? – yes. That we could accept. We had been beaten by practically everyone over the years and the quality of Dutch football in particular was renowned throughout the world. But cricket?!

Five years later at Amstelveen an England XI captained by Peter Roebuck and containing no fewer than seven internationals (Stephenson J.P., Bailey R.J., Hussain N., Watkinson M., Pringle D.R., Capel D.J. and Thomas J.G.) would lose to a Netherlands XI and in that same annus horribilis of 1989 an MCC side containing six former county cricketers would lose to France in Paris. France, for God's sake! Until that point I didn't even know they played the game. For me French cricket was that silly mutant form of the noble game you played on beaches trying to defend your legs. It scarcely deserved to go by the name 'cricket' at all. What next? Defeat perhaps in a one-day match at the hands of the mighty China as our bowlers concede over 90 no-balls for shoulder-high deliveries, or Germany catching England on a typical Düsseldorf 'Stickyhund' and rolling us over for under 100? Frankly, having seen Zimbabwe's Eddo Brandes rip through our batting, anything now seems possible, but even back in 1984 we felt that our ignominious failure was symptomatic of a defective gene running through the whole game from village cricket right up to the national team.

Cricket more than any other sport England plays resonates with politics. It stems from the imperial era when the 19th-century Nigels and Henrys of the Colonial Service played sedate games against each other to remind them of good old Blighty. Later it was used in a covert political way to help assimilate the indigenous middle classes into the English way of life. It was played in the elite public schools set up throughout the empire and was held up as a symbol of Victorian England with its ideals of fair play and gracious etiquette. To play the game of cricket was to play at being English. Not to labour the point, cricket is indivisible from any notion of Englishness. Australia, Pakistan, West Indies and South Africa all play with a verve and effectiveness of which England currently can only dream. It is these countries that set the standards for the game, yet still the yardstick of achievement is to beat England. The team everyone takes greatest pleasure in beating is England, no matter how inept we might be, for beating England at cricket is in some way self-defining.

This social and political baggage that comes with cricket also explains why just about all of mainland Europe has turned its back on the sport in total contrast to the way it embraced football. In fact cricket only really endured where there was a lasting imperial presence. In North America and the trading nations of South America the game never took root beyond the expatriate community. As proud, independent nations with their own social and cultural traditions there was no way France, Germany, Italy and the like were going to play a game that paid such homage to England and the English way of life. Their values and temperament stood in some respects in opposition to the values of cricket. You've only got to think of the way a Frenchman or an Italian drives with his total disregard for traffic regulations to picture what he would make of the honourable concepts of 'walking' or 'the umpire's decision is final'. *'Soddez cela pour un jeu de soldats!'* I hear the Frenchman cry. Or imagine a German trying to come to terms with the notion of declaring an innings closed. Not a chance. They would get up early, spread their bath towels over the pitch to claim first use of the wicket and then bat all day, refusing to let the other side have a go and hope to win on penalties in the final hour.

It is because of the very Englishness of the game that it hurts so when we fail. But thoughts of failure were far from our minds as we took the ferry from Dover to Ostend. It was a high-spirited journey as you would expect from fourteen blokes in their early twenties who had just sat two weeks of exams and now had two months off prior to joining the rat race. But that said, there is something about large groups of men denied the restraining, civilising influence of women about which I have never really felt entirely comfortable, despite playing team games all my life. Much later, when I had to attend various friends' stag nights, I would feel the same sense of unease. It really is too despairing for words to see a gaggle of grown men, all holding down sensible jobs in accountancy or banking, baying for blood as some tired old stripper humiliates the groom with the aid of some shaving foam and a bottle of iodine. And here we were, fourteen blokes on our way to Amsterdam.

Amsterdam is a kind of theme park for males with turbo-charged levels of testosterone and it was clear from very early on that Anne Frank's House and the Rijksmuseum were to be eschewed as leisure attractions in favour of the famous red light district. There, on a nightly basis, we would lurch from bar to bar before ending up in some strip joint watching some poor girl dressed in nothing but a mosquito net doing entertaining tricks with three ping pong balls. But perhaps more distressing than the fact that this was how we spent every evening, was the fact that we never tired of it.

Our itinerary gave us two days to get used to the Dutch way of life before our first match. Now, on the high plains of South Africa's *veldt*, this would have been vital if we were going to acclimatise to the high altitude, or equally in Madras we would have needed a day or two to get accustomed to the searing heat. But in low-lying, temperate Holland, where the bars stay open all day and soft drugs are legalised, it was nothing short of a disaster. All of us were in worse shape than when we had left England. Three of our number had spent the early hours in an Amsterdam police station following that misguided attempt to drive a motorised boat down a canal in the middle of the night, while another had staggered back to the hotel much the worse for wear and concussed himself on the revolving door. Best of all, one of our batsmen had gone back to the flat of someone he later discovered to be a transvestite called Bettina and was still in a state of shock the following morning as we countered hangovers with vats of coffee. In keeping with the tradition of Southampton teams, we were struggling to field eleven players, let alone eleven fit ones.

Our opening match was against a club from Rotterdam who were by their own admission one of the weaker teams in Holland and apparently missing a couple of their better players. All of which only served to fuel further our swaggering arrogance. We won the toss and batted. Our openers padded up while the rest of us looked forward to a relaxing time in the late-morning sunshine. We were about to show these Dutch fellows what cricket, and in particular English cricket, was all about and when we slumped to 26 for four I think they'd got the gist. Of course, we were merely emulating the national side when it embarks on an overseas tour. England normally get bowled out for less than a hundred by the Tobago Taxi Drivers XI, or let the Tamil Nadu Postal Workers Select XI post a score in excess of 600, but 26 for four was really rather desperate even by England's standards.

All of our early batsmen had failed to come to terms with the 'tennis ball bounce' afforded by the artificial wicket and these Dutch boys knew exactly how to bowl on it. Bang it in straight and just short of a length and it was practically impossible to get away. From pure frustration our batsmen got themselves out. These wickets were absolutely made for beefy blokes bowling straight up and down 'dobblers' which only makes me wonder all the more how an England XI with Pringle, Capel and Watkinson can have failed in that match in 1989. In the end we managed 142 and a combination of their equally poor batting and late afternoon drizzle conspired to force a draw – the sort of result that would have had David Lloyd running about barking, 'We flippin' murdered 'em!' We knew better, though, and the early swagger had definitely gone. They even had a bloke who could drink three pints of lager in under ten seconds so pride couldn't be salvaged during the post-match drinking session either.

The next match we lost miserably. They scored 220 in their 40 overs and we were bowled out for 117. Again, we were unhinged by two broad-shouldered Dutchmen pegging away short of a length and constantly hitting the splice. And so we saw the addition of a new gremlin in the complex-ridden mind of the English cricketer. For many years we have been intimidated by the mere appearance of certain cricketers. A long-limbed West Indian getting off the opposition team's coach would send a tremor through the home batting ranks. Instantly, he would be seen as the apotheosis of West Indian fast bowlers, an ebony ogre hued from the same wood as Hall, Griffiths, Roberts, Holding, Garner and Ambrose. Suddenly, batsmen numbers 1, 2 and 3 would be offering to bat down the order 'to give the other guys a chance', or they would discover a non-existent injury – a ten-minute migraine, or a tweaked hamstring putting the pads on. Waiting batsmen would whimper unashamedly as he marked out his long run and pawed the ground. Those who couldn't bear the sight of blood would lock themselves away in the toilets. But rarely would the anticipated hurricane materialise. The giant would reveal himself to be a plodding seamer and, as if by magic, migraines would disappear, hamstrings would be untweaked and the demons temporarily exorcised until the next time a lithe athletic Jamaican struts into the opposition dressing room the whole process would repeat itself. But the inferiority complex is not restricted to West Indians. All Asians no matter what shape or size are viewed with equal suspicion – a whirling dervish delivering fizzing spinners from triple-jointed digits. While a South African or Australian accent denotes a fiercely aggressive competitor who would rather bite his own arm off than shake you by the hand and wish you good luck.

I have often wondered whether this stereotyped thinking prevails in the minds of overseas cricketers. Does a South African club player see a dormant Mushtaq Ahmed in every Asian cricketer he plays against? Does an Aussie's bottom trumpet at the mere sighting of a West Indian in the car park? And what effect does an English accent have? Do they think, 'Shit, they've got an Englishman. He'll be a bloody tricky trundler.' Or, 'Hell, that English bloke will bat all day.' It's an interesting aside to try to find *the* aspect of play that is quintessentially English. With most of the other countries it's easy – a fierce bouncer (West Indies), a sharp leg spinner (Pakistan), a floating off-break (India), a brilliant diving stop (South Africa), a huge six off the first ball of the match (Sri Lanka), an impudent single (Australia), but with England the defining facets of the game seem to be the nagging seamer or the forward defensive prod. It's all revealing of a deep-rooted inferiority complex and inherent cautiousness that is now endemic in our sport. To such an extent that we had begun to fear the appearance of tall, strapping Dutchmen. 'Oh God. Here we go again,' we would mutter as some barrel-chested teenager who looked like he'd just finished summer camp with the Hitler Jugend bounded in.

One pyrrhic victory against a club's colts XI was scarcely enough to salvage pride on our tour, but things hit rock bottom in our last match. We got off to an inauspicious start when we only had five players on the ground by the time the toss took place. We lost the toss and they opted to bat but subsequently agreed to field when Ian came clean about his predicament. We were 16 for two with Ian anxiously phoning the hotel to see if the rest of his team had appeared when two taxis pulled into the ground containing some very hungover specimens. The attractions of an all-night party somewhere in the city's suburbs had proven irresistible and these wretches were paying for it now. Three were unable to assume the vertical position and so were obvious candidates to be omitted. But the others scarcely looked better. Quickly assessing the delicate health of our side, their captain, Bruce Blair, who had played one-day internationals for New Zealand, brought on the Dutch women's Under-21 team's opening bowler as first change. This was a cruel stunt to pull on blokes whose pride was already wounded only marginally less than their livers. The sheer terror of getting out to a woman rendered our batsmen practically strokeless. Ms Bochove lolloped in off a ten-yard run and bowled slowish in-swingers on a decent length. Transfixed with the fear of dismissal our batsmen prodded them back. Those in the pavilion hollered with glee as maiden after maiden was played out and it was hard to say what was more fun, the sight of Ms Bochove's run-up – a vision that requires you to imagine two bunny rabbits fighting under a travel rug – or the batsman's chauvinistic shame at not being able to score. The only one not laughing was the bloke waiting to go in and it is perhaps the only occasion in 25 years of playing that I have heard the next-in batsman praying that the fast bowlers get brought back into the attack.

After taking no chances against her for long periods three of our batsmen perished going for huge manly heaves and it was only the result of some hectic scurrying at the end, that we mustered 143 off our 40 overs. This was never going to be enough and Rupert Gomes (Larry's brother) and Bruce Blair put us out of our misery with a firework display of big hitting.

It was all a fitting climax to our tour. Thrashed in six matches and now humbled by a girlie with big in-swingers as it were. Had we warranted the attentions of the press pack that hounds England teams abroad, it would not have been difficult to predict the tabloid headlines: 'DUTCH CAP IT ALL'. 'SOUTHAMPTON ALL CLOGGED UP' etc.

In hindsight I learned very little about Aristotle, Plato, Marx and co. at university (I certainly can't remember much), but I did learn the same lesson England did on the 1996–97 trip to Zimbabwe – never underestimate your opponents, and remember, everyone wants to beat the English at cricket.

CHAPTER SEVEN

Stick to the Sandwiches
Cricket and the fairer sex

West Indies v England (3rd Test)

Date: 25–30 March 1994   *Venue:* Queen's Park Oval, Port-of-Spain, Trinidad
Toss: West Indies

West Indies

D.L.Haynes	b Salisbury	38	b Lewis		19
*R.B.Richardson	lbw b Salisbury	63	c and b Caddick		3
B.C.Lara	lbw b Lewis	43	c Salisbury b Caddick		12
K.L.T.Arthurton	lbw b Lewis	1	c Stewart b Caddick		42
J.C.Adams	c Smith b Lewis	2	c Russell b Salisbury		43
S.Chanderpaul	b Fraser	19	c Fraser b Caddick		50
†J.R.Murray	not out	27	c Russell b Caddick		14
W.K.M.Benjamin	b Fraser	10	c Fraser b Lewis		35
C.E.L.Ambrose	c Thorpe b Fraser	13	b Caddick		12
K.C.G.Benjamin	b Fraser	9	not out		5
C.A.Walsh	lbw b Lewis	0	lbw b Lewis		1
Extras	(B1, LB13, W1, NB12)	27	(B8, LB13, NB12)		33
Total		**252**			**269**

Bowling	O	M	R	W	O	M	R	W
Fraser	24	9	49	4	25	6	71	0
Caddick	19	5	43	0	26	5	65	6
Lewis	25.2	3	61	4	27.5	6	71	3
Salisbury	22	4	72	2	9	1	41	1
Ramprakash	2	1	8	0				
Hick	3	1	5	0				

England

*M.A.Atherton	c Murray b W.K.M.Benjamin	48	lbw b Ambrose		0
A.J.Stewart	b Ambrose	6	b Ambrose		18
M.R.Ramprakash	c and b W.K.M.Benjamin	23	run out		1
R.A.Smith	lbw b Ambrose	12	b Ambrose		0
G.A.Hick	lbw b Walsh	40	c Murray b Ambrose		6
G.P.Thorpe	c Lara b Ambrose	86	b Ambrose		3
†R.C.Russell	b Ambrose	23	(8)c sub (P.V.Simmons) b Ambrose		4
C.C.Lewis	b Ambrose	9	(9)c W.K.M.Benjamin b Walsh		6
I.D.K.Salisbury	c Lara b Walsh	36	(7)c Lara b Walsh		0
A.R.Caddick	c Lara b W.K.M.Benjamin	6	c Lara b Walsh		1
A.R.C.Fraser	not out	8	not out		0
Extras	(B10, LB9, W1, NB11)	31	(LB6, NB1)		7
Total		**328**			**46**

Bowling	O	M	R	W	O	M	R	W
Ambrose	29	6	60	5	10	1	24	6
Walsh	27.2	3	77	2	9.1	1	16	3
K.C.G.Benjamin	20	5	70	0				
W.K.M.Benjamin	24	3	66	3				
Adams	4	0	18	0				
Chanderpaul	5	0	13	0				
Arthurton	3	0	5	0				

We touched on the subject of the one-cap wonders a little earlier. Well, my own particular favourite of this select band is Tony Pigott who played in one Test in New Zealand in 1984, returning the unremarkable figures of two for 75 in a match made remarkable by England's failure to reach 100 in either innings. Pigott wasn't even in the tour party. He just happened to be the only professional bowler qualified for England within a taxi ride of the ground at Christchurch when Foster and Dilley were both declared unfit.

He's not completely alone in having won his cap in such circumstances. This also happened to Ken Palmer, the Somerset seamer and current umpire, who got the call-up in 1965 for his sole Test in Port Elizabeth. Pakistan, too, called upon the services of the laughably rotund Ehteshamuddin on their tour of England in 1982. A man who made Ian Austin look positively anorexic, Ehteshamuddin was so unsuited to the rigours of anything more than a club match on a Sunday afternoon, that he pulled a muscle on the second day and took no further part.

These selections sustain gloriously the rather slapdash, amateur ethic that to this day runs right through cricket. It's hard to imagine, for instance, the England football team on an overseas tour of say Latin America having to draft in Exeter City's centre-half who by chance was holidaying with his family in nearby Disneyworld. No, what happened on these occasions is exactly what happens every

Saturday all round the country. Someone drops out at the last minute, a desperate phone-round reveals everybody else is unavailable and so there's no choice but to phone that bloke from Accounts who can't play for toffee but is always keen to help out 'if you're really short'. You know the sort. You've seen him on the village green – he's the one wearing the Green Flash plimsolls and the off-white chinos who drops the ball every time someone throws it to him. Tony Pigott is this man's spiritual ancestor.

But I also single these three out because they exemplify every cricket fan's ultimate fantasy – to be plucked from obscurity in his country's hour of greatest need and, unlike Pigott and co., to put in a match-winning performance that turns the whole series round. I've had this fantasy since I was eight. It varies slightly according to my mood and the prevailing circumstances but broadly it follows the same general plot. There's a mounting injury crisis. I'm the only feasible candidate and get called up five minutes before the toss. I make my debut and soon England are in dire straits at 37 for six. (As you can see, it's a fantasy with its roots very much in reality.) I go in at number 8 and play the innings of a lifetime hitting Ambrose for six, reverse sweeping Walsh. I score a huge hundred and England reach the respectability of 300-odd. Greenidge and Haynes then deal savagely with our new ball bowlers until at 150 for nought the skipper asks if I'd like to turn my arm over. I go on to break Jim Laker's bowling record of 19 wickets in a match and we beat them by an innings inside two days.

We've all had this fantasy but as I packed my suitcase in March 1994 on the eve of our departure to the Caribbean, where my girlfriend, Fran, and I were going for a three-week holiday, the fantasy came to me stronger and more vividly than ever before, because it occurred to me: 'I could be the next Tony Pigott.'

In fact, the more I thought about it the more I convinced myself my call-up was imminent. Well, there weren't going to be that many Englishmen in Trinidad. A couple of thousand at the most. Take away all those over the age of 50, and all those who haven't played since school and you're down to a few hundred. Then assume a rare tropical illness sweeps through the press box denying the tour selectors the option of drafting in former players. And finally, discount all those who have not got their own kit and there couldn't be more than a handful left from which to choose. From this point, it certainly wasn't hard to imagine the cricketing circumstances falling into place. Phil Tufnell goes AWOL and Ian Salisbury is put down. It looks like the wicket will turn and there's no way they can go in with just Hicky's part-time lollipops. Mercifully, they can't fly Embers out in time. So they're stuffed. Where can they find a spinner who can bat a bit and won't let them down in the field? The fantasy is in full swing.

I feel a tap on my shoulder. I turn round and it is Athers. 'Bus, thank God you're here. You're playing.'

'But, Mike . . .'

'No buts, mate. It's going to turn square out there. We need someone who'll give it some rip. Have you brought your kit?'

'Of course. I never go anywhere without it.'

You see it's easy to imagine how it could happen. Well, it is for the deluded cricket-obsessed male. But unfortunately, women don't understand this sort of thinking and it is just at the moment when I was putting my folded cricket whites into my case that Fran entered the bedroom. 'What are you packing those for?'

'What?'

'Your cricket stuff. God, I thought you were only watching it. You're not playing it as well!?'

'No, no. It's just . . . well, you never know. Someone might offer me a game.'

'Like who?'

'Er . . . England.'

'England?! They're not that bad, are they?'

'No, but injuries . . . tropical illnesses. You never know.'

'Look, I thought we agreed this. You're going to the cricket in Trinidad and Barbados. The rest of the time we do what I want to do.'

'Fine. Fine. But . . .'

'But what?'

'It happened to Tony Pigott.'

'What did?'

'Nothing.'

'I think it's better if we leave these behind.' And with that she grabbed my neatly folded whites from the suitcase and stuffed them back into an open drawer.

Twelve hours later we were sitting on a BWIA 747 bound for the Caribbean. We were both very excited but for different reasons. For her it was all golden sands, an azure blue sea and rum punches under a starlit sky. For me it was Athers and the boys facing Curtly and co. on a Port-of-Spain sticky dog and as I pondered about the three weeks ahead of us and on the cricket whites episode of the night before I realised that I was about to embark on a voyage of experience that would test to the full the compatibility of my two loves – cricket and Fran.

You don't have to be Desmond Morris to work out that men and women need each other. Men have a strong biological drive to seek out women and more importantly to copulate with them. On the other hand, women need men to connect up their stereos. Thus our gender destinies are inextricably linked. But despite this mutuality it is not uncommon for the two sexes to diverge quite radically on a number of issues. The male infatuation with sport and in particular, cricket, is one such issue.

Basically, most women don't see the point of sport. But what worries them more is that men do. Perhaps worse, not only do men see the point of sport but it exerts an all-engulfing hold on them to the exclusion of everything that in turn women seem to hold dear, like relationships, marriages, family, that sort of guff. Any woman involved with a cricket fanatic soon realises that if she tells him she heard on the radio that Mark Ramprakash has been picked for England again this will provoke a volley of expletives, much throwing of arms to the sky, and occasional banging of cranium on the wall. But if she announces that her gynaecologist has informed her she must have her womb scraped she'll be lucky to get a consoling 'oh dear'. Far more likely is the response: 'When? I hope not Thursday. It's India at The Oval.'

The problem is one of conflicting value systems. Just take my friend, Andrew, whose wife's waters broke during the Headingley Test of 1981 and with Australia at 109 for seven. There were England staging one of the most remarkable fightbacks in history and here was his wife flooding the sitting room. She was all for going to the hospital right away. He was all for waiting until the contractions had started (or until the match was over – whichever was the sooner).

Genuine sexual harmony will only be possible when women come to terms with one fundamental truth: men *are* capable and indeed frequently *do* form meaningful, loving relationships with women but deep down, no matter how often he might tell her he loves her, there always lurks the chance that some curvy chick who laughs at his jokes will come along and she'll be, as Devon would have it, 'history'. Whereas a relationship with a cricket team is *permanent*.

This may sound sick that a man can be more committed to a troop of flannelled fools than he is to his own wife or girlfriend but it's important to bear in mind the bigger picture from the bloke's perspective. His wife/girlfriend may be affectionate, devoted and good company, but there is no way she is ever going to win the AXA Equity and Law League. At least not until she perfects those sliding stops in the outfield and learns to take those quick singles. But there is every chance that if a bloke keeps faithful his team might, just might, do it and, if he's really good, win the championship too.

You've only got to look at those Warwickshire fans. For years they put up with the likes of Neil Abberley, Norman McVicker, Geoff Humpage and Anton Ferreira, and then suddenly, a bonanza – they win the treble. The treble! Championship, Sunday League and Benson and Hedges Cup. Now unless your girlfriend is Sharon Stone and she likes to dribble cling peaches over your privates every night you'll never get that sort of thrill from a woman. Moreover, when your girlfriend/wife is 60 and has long since exchanged the skimpy black lacy numbers for something that looks more like it was built by Harland and Wolff, and would rather give blood than head on the basis that at least she gets a cup of tea and a plate of custard creams after, you'll still have the boys in white. And in turn they'll still have you.

These relationships with teams are unconditional too. There are no strings attached as there are with human ones. A team demands nothing more of you than blind loyalty and in return it will try to reward you with some level of cricketing competence but with a woman it is a far more complex affair. It's apparently not just enough to love her, you've got to like her friends, put up with her mother, indulge her father and his passion for home brewing, and enjoy visiting garden centres. All this and she still has the nerve to accuse you of being more interested in Ceefax than her. No, it was clear that there was much to be done to bridge the sporting chasm between us and this holiday was as good a time as any to start.

It was the first time I'd followed England overseas; a pursuit I had always presumed was only within the budget and timetable of the idle rich. There were, however, all sorts on our chartered plane – pensioners, school teachers taking advantage of the Easter holidays, and lots of cricket anorak types called Derek or Graham who were invariably computer programmers or insurance loss adjusters. I was struck by the fact that if this plane were to crash into the Atlantic, anything up to 80 per cent of the world's recorded production of velcro-fastening shoes would go down with it.

Fran read her book during most of the flight. I became embroiled in conversation with Bob, a local government officer from Blackburn, who was sitting next to me. Bob was a lifelong Lancashire supporter who had devoted the last ten winters to watching England lose overseas. He was an old hand at this touring game and took enormous pleasure in sharing with me the highs and lows of his travels. It was a travelogue of cricket facts and figures punctuated with the most bizarre observations about the various countries visited. New Zealand was described as 'very clean and a bit like Scotland, only without the drunks. You'll not find people urinating in multi-storey car parks in Dunedin,' Bob pronounced. As for India, he was struck by how kind the Indian people were, though he bemoaned the fact that 'they had no control over their cows. They just let them wander all over the place and nobody does a thing.' I tried to point out gently that the cow has great symbolic meaning in Hinduism, but I could sense that this did not wash with Bob. Sacred cows or not, the whole thing offended his standards of order and decency; standards that he had stringently applied for many years on behalf of the good burghers of Blackburn. There's no way Bob would have allowed a herd of Friesians to graze in Blackburn's civic centre, trampling all over the putting green, munching on the ornamental clock. Absolutely not.

Australia was liked but considered pricey. He'd once had a cappuccino in Perth that cost £3.60. In fact, Bob was so shocked at the price that he took a photograph of the bill. I could not help but picture the misery of Bob's colleagues at work as every year he returned from the chemist's with his holiday snaps. 'This is my hotel . . . and this my room. You can see the tea-making facility in the corner.'

Sri Lanka was cheap in contrast, but was I aware that state television there was showing episodes of *Kojak*? And so it went on for seven long hours. One of Bob's jobs at Blackburn council was to coordinate a civil defence programme in response to a nuclear attack. Suffice it to say that most people would find a nuclear holocaust preferable to being stuck down a bunker with Bob – unless of course they were interested in knowing facts like where Farokh Engineer gets his hair cut or how much it costs to hire a moped in St Lucia. I looked at Fran who I noticed was wearing her headphones even though they weren't plugged into the arm rest. Occasionally she cast a thunderous look in Bob's direction. I sensed they weren't going to get on . . .

During the few blissful minutes while Bob disappeared to 'spend a penny' (mind you, it cost him 20p in Brisbane once, you know), I tried to entertain Fran. I pointed out the elbow which was perched on the arm rest of the seat two rows in front of me and explained it belonged to Tom Graveney and how that illustrious elbow was a key component in the execution of one of the sport's most sumptuous cover drives. She mustered a look of something some way short of indifference and then countered with a long description of the precise technique used by generations of Chinese women to bind their feet (what they would have done for velcro-fasteners!) Still, Fran had made her intentions plain. She was only 70 pages into a huge tome entitled *Wild Swans* by Jung Chang about Chinese women, love and chiropody, and had all the ammunition required to match my cricketing whimsy. Whether she could have coped with Bob on a roll was, however, another thing entirely.

Tom Graveney's elbow was the first of many brushes with cricketing celebrity that Fran and I were to have over the three weeks and each one she met with the same stoic indifference. Ever since I was nine and stood behind Wendy Craig in a post office queue I have been amused by such juxtapositions of the famous and the banal. My all-time favourite is that of a friend of mine, an actor and comedian, who returned from the gents toilets at the Crucible Theatre, Sheffield, and announced with some pride that he'd just shared a hand drier with Doug Mountjoy; though the aunt who claims she once sat on a bar stool still warm from the bottom of *Family Fortunes* host Les Dennis must come a close second.

This holiday, however, was to afford me with all manner of such encounters. In the hotel in Barbados I passed a bowl of Frosties to Alec Stewart the day before he went on to score the first of his two centuries. In Grenada I chatted to Vic Marks about the scarcity of sun loungers by the pool, and in Trinidad Fran and I shared a lift with Alan Igglesden. Iggy asked us what floor we wanted. I told him and he pressed the appropriate buttons. One of those awful lift silences ensued, so I felt compelled to reopen conversation. 'How's the back, Alan?' I asked. I had toyed briefly with 'Iggy' and even 'Al' but I was pleased that 'Alan' seemed to strike the right note of polite informality. 'Not great,' he revealed. The door opened and he got out. Scarcely the stuff of Wilde and Whistler but it had confirmed my worst fears – I should have packed my kit. 'See!' I growled at Fran. 'It'll be Tony Pigott all over again.'

Generalisation though it is, women seem far less impressed by these brief encounters with the good and the great. Idolatry is not their thing. In my experience they don't have heroes. Well, not in the same way men do. Fran is a fan of Jill Tweedie, the late feminist writer and *Guardian* columnist, but she doesn't know where Jill was born, what school she went to, what her favourite food is, and who in the whole world she would most like to meet. Let alone her career batting average. Blokes on the other hand make it their business to know these things (and more). To this day I could reel off all Graham Thorpe's scores in his entire Test career. I could tell you the name of John Edrich's first wife. Or the birthplace of Younis Ahmed. How I know these things, or even why, I don't know. I just do. But women don't seem to have time for these important details. And more fool them, I say. I would like to see your average female deal with an uncomfortable longueur in a lift as it gets stuck between floors – especially if it was say, John Edrich, in the lift with them. They would be bereft of conversation whereas I could break the ice by asking John if he still kept in touch with Valerie.

This sort of trivia is meaningless to women. They just can't see the point of it. Not so long ago, I returned home from work delighted with my discovery on the tube that Finsbury Park spelt backwards is Krapy Rubsnif. Now this had kept me amused for 20 minutes but it scarcely raised a titter from Fran who seemed far more interested in clearing a blocked drain outside the kitchen with some rods.

*   *   *

154

We were staying in the Port-of-Spain Hilton which for the architecturally curious of you is built upside down on a hill; i.e. the reception is on the top floor which means you go *down* to the bedrooms. It may be an award-winning design but it is also sodding confusing after nine bottles of Carib.

Both teams and the gentlemen of the media were staying there along with a growing number of the polyester faithful from England. Mercifully, Bob was not staying in our hotel but in a local bed and breakfast. He took great delight in informing us that he had checked with the hotel and it was perfectly all right with them if he wanted to use its facilities. So, according to his calculations, he was saving £87.42 a night. 'I'll see you round the pool,' he boomed insensitively, 'the first round is on me.' Fran was developing an Inspector Dreyfus-style pathological hatred of Bob. I realised the less she saw of him the better – if only for his sake. So when he started to show us his food supplies from home – Dairy Lea cheese triangles, packets of Penguin biscuits, PG Tips, dried skimmed milk etc. – explaining that since his nasty experience with a kebab in Faisalabad he took no risks with food overseas. I decided to usher Bob away to safety and leave Fran alone to regain her composure.

Noticeably, however, Bob's cautious attitude to the local cuisine was shared by the England team. As we dined in the hotel restaurant on Callaloo soup, a thick green sludge of spinach and nutmeg, followed by curried goat, our boys were picking at pizzas. Somehow this unwillingness to embrace the local culture gets to the heart of England's problems when touring, namely the siege mentality that they seem to develop. Be it the media, the hot weather, the travelling arrangements or the local playing conditions, they seem to think everything is against them and so they turn inwards and hanker after home comforts. Mike Gatting famously never toured without his own private store of Branston pickle and Phil Tufnell while in India in 1993 allegedly declined to visit the Taj Mahal on the basis that it was 'just another fucking temple'. You can't help but feel that if the players stopped viewing overseas tours as an unwelcome dollop of community service imposed on them by vindictive selectors, the three-nil defeats abroad might not have become such a time-honoured ritual.

The following morning, Fran sought out the nearest beach, while I traipsed down to the Queen's Park Oval to watch the teams practise. The West Indies team bedecked in maroon tracksuits went through a routine of callisthenics; stretching exercises, gentle jogging and then some time later had a net. Meanwhile, England players fielded rolling balls before throwing them into Geoff Arnold's baseball mitt and Keith Fletcher displayed all his prowess of old by nicking catches to a posse of slip fielders. The West Indies practised as a tight unit. England were strewn all over the outfield standing huddled together in groups waiting to field a rolling ball. It was all eerily reminiscent of the way most village or club sides 'warm up'. It normally opens with the few who arrived at the ground already changed throwing some shoulder-wrenching 'skiers' to each other. Then once fingers have been bruised and battered and any confidence of ever catching one completely expunged, the wicket-keeper waddles on in full regalia and demands hard, flat, skimming throws. These invariably reach him on the half volley endangering the recent bridgework to his upper set, or they clear him by a full ten feet. Those that do reach him at the optimum height, he drops. Others practise their occasional leg-spin to the side of the wicket, although some berk can never resist trying to uproot the virgin stumps with his 'quicker ball', while the opening bowler marks out his full run, steams in and bowls a slinging wide one that cracks some unsuspecting wretch on the ankle. In short, it's a shambles and I am afraid similar impressions were formed about England's preparations.

That night I couldn't sleep and it wasn't just because of the squadron of mosquitoes that were patrolling the skies of our bedroom. In-built within the British sporting psyche is a natural inferiority complex especially when it comes to cricket. In all but the rarest of circumstances I want the team I am playing for or supporting to bat second. This is based on the loser's principle that the opposition is so obviously better than us that if we bat first it could be all over in 40 minutes. Whereas if they bat first, get a bucketful, and then bowl us out for 12 at least we've all had a nice day out.

The 'nice day out syndrome' often goes hand in hand with the equally weedy 'let's make a game of it'. Dave 'one shot' Sheridan (an elegant player off the front foot who if you placed a long-off or long-on from the outset would be starved of runs or caught on the boundary trying to clear him) and I once played in a match against The Blue Angel in Henley. They batted first and within 15 minutes our opening bowlers had reduced them to five for seven. At that point our skipper made the grand gesture of deciding we should 'make a game of it' rather than risk the prospect of the dreaded beer match. He brought Dave, very much a non-bowler, and our wicket-keeper on to bowl and soon their score had climbed to the relatively lofty heights of 67 before their last man succumbed to a wild smear across the line. A desultory 68 were needed. We fell 32 runs short – all out for 35. Dave caught at long-off for 3.

As the squadron leader led his bloodthirsty chaps in for yet another raid, I found myself praying England would have to bat second. It was a long way to come to watch England bowled out for 40-odd in the first innings. Ha, if only I had known.

My prayers were answered. On arrival at the ground it was announced that Richardson had won the toss and the West Indies were batting. Fran and I settled into our seats in the Jeffrey Stollmeyer stand and savoured the distinctive Caribbean atmosphere. Conch shells, whistles and bells competed with the cries of the peanut sellers; one of whom, a Rastafarian by the name of Jambo, performed his party piece of hurling packets of nuts to his assistants 40 or 50 yards away in the back of the stands and never missing. It was a performance in stark contrast to the England fielding practice the day before. All around there was constant chatter, shrieks of joy when boundaries were hit, oohs and ahhs when bouncers went through and all the action took place against the verdant backdrop of the mountains and the deep blue Caribbean Sea.

We had pre-paid tickets organised as part of the holiday package and so we sat in a block mostly populated by Brits sheltering under those trademark British white sunhats. These shapeless blobs of cotton/nylon mix are cleverly designed to provide protection for the head but not quite enough for the average Englishman's proboscis. The result is the dream ticket of pasty complexion and fluorescent pink nose. This, coupled with the sandals and terylene socks, the Cecil Rhodes shorts, and a sickly coconut whiff of Timothy White's suncream is proof perfect once again why you would back Lorenzo, Philippe, or even Stavros ahead of Darren in the Intertotty Cup at Fuenteventura every summer. Something goes horribly wrong when the middle-aged Brit has to make decisions about leisurewear. It is a British disease. I am still haunted by the footage of John and Norma Major on holiday with ex-Prime Minister Gonzales of Spain and his wife. There they were cavorting about the Med in a dinghy: Gonzales looking laid back and smooth in Timberlands, shorts and polo shirt while our John was throwing himself into the holiday spirit by wearing suit trousers and a pin-stripe shirt. His one concession to being on holiday was to slip off his suit jacket and not wear a tie. Racey, eh?

It was hot and muggy, which seemed to make the smells of freshly prepared rotis and the chickens frying in large skillets behind the ground linger all the more seductively in the air. It looked business as usual on the pitch. Atherton had dropped a sitter off Fraser, who typically looked like he was on the verge of a coronary after one delivery, and Haynes and Richardson had tripped along merrily for an opening stand of 66. Then England got lucky. Haynes missed Salisbury's stock ball – the full toss – and was bowled. A delightful but thankfully brief cameo from Lara followed and then Salisbury snared Richardson with his 'other ball' – the long hop. Disciplined bowling and the West Indies' predilection to press the self-destruct button made for a great day's play littered with West Indian wickets. As I leapt out of my chair, cheered every wicket, and performed self-consciously uncool high fives with England fans around me, Fran hardly made a squeak. Through all this she read, dozed in the sun, went off for strolls, licked at ice-creams, and listened to her Walkman. Occasionally, she would ask what happened when a wicket fell, or what time tea was, or that most irritating of questions: 'Who's winning?' Where was Bob in my hour of need? Frankly, I would have willingly traded her in for someone who knew their cricketing onions. But then I caught sight of Bob some ten rows away in animated conversation with the poor devil next to him. I could just imagine the scene: 'Did I tell you Bernard Reidy's mother lives four doors away from me?' Bob or Fran – it was a tough call. But I fancied I'd just about called correctly.

The game unfolded over the next three days with England

constantly on top. Thorpe's 86 in the first innings and a few hefty blows from the tail made sure of a useful lead of 76. We never imagined the West Indies would bat as sloppily as they did first time round, but they did. The top three were dismissed before the deficit was rubbed out and though Arthurton and Adams played well, neither of them went on to make a big score. The real bonus came in the last over of the day. It was a clever move by Atherton to bring on Salisbury with the batsmen focused solely on defence. How could they resist six consecutive strawberries from him? The spinner's art is to get the batsman in two minds by changes of pace, flight and turn. Salisbury gets batsmen in two minds by a wholly different method – he lobs them up and they don't know whether to hit them for four or six. It is a costly method but about every three years it works and this is exactly how Jimmy Adams fell to the fifth ball of the last over. A wide leg-side long hop was swept fiercely at the ducking Robin Smith at forward short leg. The ball creamed into his upper arm and popped up for Russell to nip round and complete the catch. A celebratory wardance took place in the stand, and I hugged and kissed Fran who was both surprised by this spontaneous act of affection and somewhat put out since she dropped her book and lost her place. Only 91 ahead, with all their recognised batsmen gone, and just the diminutive debutant Chanderpaul and the tail to come.

England were on the threshold of victory and to ape Max Boyce – 'I was there.' It was too thrilling. That night we went out to a restaurant in the hills. We dined on swordfish and plantain and afterwards drank rum punches on the terrace. The lights of Port-of-Spain twinkled in the valley below us. It was a hot and balmy evening with just the hint of a breeze carrying the sweet scents of the nearby wood. Fran took my hand. I closed my eyes and sighed.

'What are you thinking?' she asked softly, squeezing my hand a little harder.

'Oh, nothing,' I muttered.

'No, go on. Tell me,' she persisted.

'No, I can't.'

'Tell me,' she whispered in my ear.

'I'm thinking that . . . well, I'm thinking . . .'

'What, darling?'

'I'm thinking that if we can keep them down to a lead of 120 to 130 we've really got a chance.'

'Oh for God's sake!' she said, letting go of my hand.

'No. It's true. There's uneven bounce. It's starting to keep low . . .'

'Oh, piss off!'

She got up and went into the restaurant. All rather odd, I thought. I put it down to the sun. I had told her not to overdo it.

This was the angriest I had seen her since I foolishly shouted out 'Jack Ikin' while making love. It's common practice, apparently, to think of dull things during intercourse in order to delay ejaculation. But somebody had set me the task of naming six England Test players since the war whose surname began with the letter 'I' and it had been bothering me for some time that I had only five.

The fourth day's play was one of the worst days of my life. Everything that could go wrong, did. Fran seemed a little tetchy. I advised plenty of fluids to ward off the funny turn of the previous night. By this I meant mineral water, but I noticed she'd drunk three rum punches by lunchtime. On the field Hick dropped Chanderpaul twice as he chiselled out a gritty 50, while Winston Benjamin scythed our suddenly wayward bowlers to all parts of the ground. It was awful to watch. There was this familiar ache in the pit of the stomach that once again the game was slipping away from us. For the first time in the whole match, Fran seemed to be taking an active interest in proceedings but I thought she showed poor judgement in how to express it. She cheered when West Indians hit boundaries and laughed when Englishmen dropped catches and frankly this behaviour was most unbecoming. I was imploring her to consider the feelings of others when at last Lewis won his second LBW appeal against Walsh in the match and the West Indies second innings was over. They had clawed their way to an awkward lead of 193.

It was never going to be easy but things were not helped by the advent of an hour-long shower that freshened up the wicket and left a nasty session of 25 overs or so for Ambrose and Walsh to do their stuff. But what was to unfold surpassed even my naturally gloomy expectations. Atherton was trapped in front first ball to one that hardly got up and umpire Steve Bucknor's digit of death was slowly raised. The crowd went wild and it was clear that Ambrose was, as Tony Greig would have it, 'on fire'. Enter Mark Ramprakash, that most startled of roadside rabbits, who in the same over proceeded to run himself out going for a second down to fine-leg. Smith didn't get forward properly and Hick, England's chocolate fireguard in the middle-order, edged tamely behind. We were 21 for four. 'Time to make a game of it,' an Englishman might have thought. Put on Haynes and Lara and let England score a few but I'm afraid Johnny Foreigner doesn't think like us. First Stewart and then Thorpe were bowled by Ambrose and England were 27 for six. Worse still, Fran was laughing hysterically.

We blokes spend most of our lives believing that, unlike women, we are able to apply logic and reason to moments of crisis. We are not governed by feelings or hormonal flushes but by rational thought. That's why when girls blub senselessly during a movie like *Bambi*, we feel obliged to point out: 'It's a cartoon deer, for Christ's sake. It's a bloody drawing! It is *only* a movie.' But when Thorpe made his way back to the pavilion with head bowed and West Indian supporters hollering for joy all around I found myself wanting to blub. And if anyone had been foolish enough to assert that 'it was only a game', I would have punched them on the nose.

Fran had proven a completely unsuitable cricket companion. She lacked the necessary blind loyalty, the willingness to be pessimistic at every stage of the match, and the ability to form wild and inconsistent prejudices. But the experience also taught me that this was not her fault. I mean what does cricket offer young women? Football at least offers glamour boys like Ryan Giggs or Jamie Redknapp. Rugby has Will Carling and his thighs. Tennis has Andre Agassi and his chest hair. Cricket has Tom Graveney's elbow. Not much of a contest there.

I suppose that as far as women are concerned, cricket is just not sexy. Worse still, it can also have a detrimental effect on your sex life and that's not just because the TV highlights are on so late these days. No, it appears that my libido is inextricably linked to the performance of the England cricket team. For long periods during the summer and shorter periods during the winter, I am amorously listless and inattentive to the emotional and physical needs of my partner. It's all very cocoa and pyjamas. Then Darren Gough takes five wickets or Alec Stewart scores a hundred and suddenly the champagne and condoms are out.

The summer of 1995 was a particularly confusing time for me and Fran, with crushing defeats at Headingley and Edgbaston followed by stirring victories at Lord's and Old Trafford. One week she'd be sleeping with Casanova, the next week it might just as well have been a Vauxhall Nova for all the love and affection she got.

But despite the obvious lack of appeal the game has for women I do have this heartfelt plea to them: make the effort to understand us more because we *are* worth it. When we're slumped on the sofa surrounded by beer cans watching the Test match, purge your mind of contempt and hold that barbed tongue, because it is possible, by taking the time to learn and understand the nuances of something that we revere, that you too will become a richer person. And by giving us the time and space to indulge ourselves, so in turn we will slowly, step by step, try to change and become more aware of your feelings within the context of a mature and understanding relationship.

But not until the Test series is over.

CHAPTER EIGHT

A View from the Sofa
The cricket media

England v West Indies (3rd Test)

Date: 6–8 July 1995   *Venue:* Edgbaston, Birmingham   *Toss:* England

England

*M.A.Atherton	c Murray b Ambrose	0	b Walsh		4
†A.J.Stewart	lbw b Benjamin	37	absent hurt		0
G.A.Hick	c Richardson b Walsh	3	c Hooper b Bishop		3
G.P.Thorpe	c Campbell b Ambrose	30	c Murray b Bishop		0
R.A.Smith	c Arthurton b Bishop	46	(2)b Bishop		41
J.E.R.Gallian	b Benjamin	7	(7)c Murray b Walsh		0
D.G.Cork	lbw b Walsh	4	(5)c sub (S.C.Williams) b Walsh		16
D.Gough	c Arthurton b Bishop	1	c Campbell b Walsh		12
P.J.Martin	c sub (S.C.Williams) b Walsh	1	(6)lbw b Walsh		0
R.K.Illingworth	b Bishop	0	(9)c Hooper b Bishop		0
A.R.C.Fraser	not out	0	(10)not out		1
Extras	(LB4, W4, NB10)	18	(NB12)		12
Total		**147**			**89**

Bowling	O	M	R	W		O	M	R	W
Ambrose	7.5	1	26	2					
Walsh	17.1	4	54	3		15	2	45	5
Bishop	6.2	0	18	3		13	3	29	4
Benjamin	13	4	45	2		2	0	15	0

West Indies

C.L.Hooper	c Stewart b Cork	40
S.L.Campbell	b Cork	79
B.C.Lara	lbw b Cork	21
J.C.Adams	lbw b Cork	10
*R.B.Richardson	b Fraser	69
K.L.T.Arthurton	lbw b Fraser	8
†J.R.Murray	c Stewart b Martin	26
I.R.Bishop	c Martin b Illingworth	16
K.C.G.Benjamin	run out	11
C.A.Walsh	run out	0
C.E.L.Ambrose	not out	4
Extras	(B5, LB5, NB6)	16
Total		**300**

Bowling	O	M	R	W
Fraser	31	7	93	2
Gough	18	3	68	0
Cork	22	5	69	4
Martin	19	5	49	1
Illingworth	8	4	11	1

It is 10.30 a.m. and the television is on. Richard and Judy are talking to a caller from Bolton about her cystitis. A detailed discussion ensues about the healing properties of natural yoghurt. I turn over. Anne and Nick are talking to Christopher Biggins. I turn over. BBC2 has a man with a beard, flared trousers and a tanktop telling me that $X=P^2$ x $3 - Y$ x A/B. I have to agree with him and try Channel Four where a man called Geraldo is talking to three lesbians who have all killed their lovers' husbands with a bicycle pump. Talk, talk, talk. Everywhere there is talk but nobody to tell me the important business of today: who has won the toss, what the wicket is looking like, who has been left out, etc. It is 15 minutes before *Test Match Special* comes on air and a whole 25 minutes before the stirring calypso signature music of the BBC's cricket coverage will be heard.

I try Ceefax. What did we do before Ceefax? Have conversations with our loved ones, I suppose. Anyway, Ceefax has no news. 'Scores will appear here', it says. Now I can't get rid of the text. It won't move. I can't get a picture. I try all kinds of angles. Close up. From the side. Even taking it by surprise. The batteries in the remote have gone. I'll never get down the shops and back in time. Ah, no, I scamper upstairs and remove two batteries from the alarm clock. Normal service has been restored. Text removed, I flick around the channels again. Two lesbians are now shouting at each other. Tanktop is still splitting the atom. Christopher Biggins has just been joined on the sofa by Su Pollard. And Lesley from Chislehurst has thrush.

I look anxiously at my watch and crack open the first beer of the day. It is Thursday 6 July 1995, the first morning of the third Test between England and West Indies at Edgbaston. The series is all square, England having won a famous victory at Lord's with Cork taking seven for 53 on his debut. I try BBC1 again. Why are these two on together? Is it National Daft Glasses Week or something?

It's 10.40. I give the radio a go. Bloody hell, it's still *Woman's Hour* and it's Jeanette Winterson being interviewed again. Well, that explains why she wasn't on Channel Four anyway – prior engagement. I pace a little. I try to relieve the suspense by performing a replica of Alec Stewart's full-stretch catch off Gough to dismiss Lara on the final morning of that Lord's Test by diving on to the sofa. Ouch!! I just tweaked my shoulder. Should have warmed up properly.

The phone rings. Bugger. I'm throwing a sicky, you see. I phoned up earlier and left a message with the switchboard. Food poisoning. Suspect chicken kebab. The phone keeps ringing. Wait. Don't pick it up yet. Here I come staggering out of the bedroom, dragging my weak, lifeless body to the phone. God I look terrible. But not as bad as I sound. 'Hello?' I half croak, half groan. I am really pleased with the effect. It strikes just the right note of sleepy feebleness. Just as well, too. It's work. 'Chicken kebab,' I whimper. 'I've been up all night . . . I'm sorry we'll have to cancel it. Can you rearrange . . . I know I've got a script to write but I'm ill . . . I don't know. Maybe I'll be feeling well enough tomorrow. [Hah. If England are doing well you can forget it.] . . . OK, well, thanks for ringing . . . No, I just wish I could get rid of this nauseousness . . .'

Then suddenly, as bold as brass, the bloody cricket music

starts blaring out. Where's the sodding remote?! Where is it?! I find it, turn it down and get back to my Oscar-winning performance on the phone. 'No, it was the telly. I think there must be some cricket match on. Anyway, look, don't worry about me. I'll be OK. Bye.'

Did I lay it on too thick? Oh, who gives a shit anyway? I worked all over Easter and not a word of thanks. Still, I've laid the foundations for tomorrow's absence if things go well. That's the trouble with cricket lasting five days. It's got to be an illness to get you off until the following Tuesday. It's like when you were a schoolkid and you threw a sicky on a Wednesday and spent the afternoon watching *Crown Court*. Your sore throat had to have turned into whooping cough, if you were going to get to see the verdict on Friday.

Sound restored and I am greeted matily by two eyebrows in a blazer that go by the name of Tony Lewis. Next to him is Geoff Boycott grinning at the camera through a triangular mouth. He is sitting bolt upright and with a faintly startled look in his eye as if Wendy Wimbush has just caught his gonads in the zipper of her pencil case. Pleasantries are exchanged and the gentle banter commences before cutting to a recording of the toss. This is what we should have been watching 20 minutes ago. Not Angela from Croydon's vaginal warts or Su Pollard's recipe for ratatouille.

Once the platitudinous interviews with the captains are over, teamsheets are confirmed and then our Geoffrey takes us on a tour of the wicket in question. We find out important stuff like how much grass has been left on, the moisture level of the soil, the state of any cracks, whether it will seam, turn, swing, or bounce. When Tony Greig did all this on Australian TV he went one step further and took out a weird Heath Robinsonesque contraption that could even gauge what they called 'the players' comfort level'. How this was measured we were never told. Small sensors located in the wicket-keeper's jockstrap perhaps? Or the temperature of the day in celsius divided by Tony's IQ? Who knows? But the real joy of our Geoff's *pièce de resistance* is that it gives us a chance to see in close-up his extraordinarily tasteless shoe collection. Will it be the black and grey lace-ups with the white socks? Or those horrid, sandy coloured slip-ons? Or, best of all, the revolting white slip-ons – the sort only hotel cocktail bar crooners or pimps wear. This is always one of my favourite moments in the build-up to a Test match and frankly is the sort of information that Ceefax should be carrying.

Then it's back to the eyebrows for a few more words with Geoffrey before the climax of this part of the day – the moment the eyebrows hand us over to Richie in the commentary box and . . . 'Mornin' everyone'. This brings us to the end of that action-packed half-hour that precedes the start of every Test match and which has become one of the features of my summers. Primed and ready to go, now the real business of the match can begin.

England have won the toss and are batting. Atherton takes guard and Ambrose marks out his run. He sets off, a tangle of limbs, like a giraffe running for a bus and bowls it fast and short. It comfortably clears the ducking Atherton as well as the leaping Junior Murray and goes for four wides. I sit back in my chair in horror. 'We're fucked,' I mumble. The fourth ball leaps off a length, takes the edge, and is caught by Murray. Atherton is out for 0. 'We're really fucked.'

Many of these commentators have been with us for years. They are like great uncles. We have known them for a long time and in a way grown quite fond of them, but they've got some very irritating habits and a dreadful tendency to talk about the good old days. You see old cricketers never die – they just join the media circus. But while the mythology of English cricket leads us to view the post-war era as a golden one, a closer inspection proves it was anything but, and some of these veterans should perhaps be more mindful of their own mishaps and inadequacies when casting aspersions on the players of today. Let's take a quick gander at the record of Great Uncle Denis, who was frequently wheeled out by the media to pour scorn on the latest embarrassing defeat. Now there are few who would question Compton's right to be considered one of the greatest batsmen of his time, but even with his masterful skills, it is interesting to note that Great Uncle Denis played in three series against Australia between 1946 and 1951 and we lost them all, 3–0, 4–0 and 4–1. In short, a record remarkably similar to today's team. And it is with no joy that I report England's propensity for batting collapses was just as strong in Compton's time. For, in one of those Ashes matches, an England team containing Hutton, Denis himself, and Bill Edrich were skittled for just 52. I wonder if the words 'fiasco' and 'national disgrace' were bandied around quite so readily then?

Uncle Trevor is another quick off the mark with a barbed comment and yet he played in an England side that lost seven Tests on the trot. But the real master of this amnesiac bloodletting is Uncle Fred who perhaps more than anybody else symbolises the generation gap in English cricket. For those people (who are probably now 50 years old or more) lucky enough to see F.S.Trueman bowl in the flesh, Fred is the apotheosis of hostile fast bowling: the glorious harnessing of a working-class labourer's physique – broad shouldered, legs like tree trunks and a big heart – with a perfect, smooth-as-mother's-dripping bowling action. But for those of us whose appreciation of his talent is limited to black and white newsreel, Uncle Fred is a cantankerous old misanthrope who should stop boring the pants off us all with his constant carping. I just hope that when England and Fred were losing 4–0 to Australia in 1958–59, or 3–1 at home to the West Indies in 1963, that someone somewhere was spluttering down a microphone: 'Well, I just don't understand what's goin' on out there.'

Fred is getting a bit long in the tooth these days and he tends now to get dragged out for the Headingley Test and maybe the one at Lord's. There's a new kid on the block now who suffers from the same problems of selective memory and that's Sky TV hardman Bob Willis. (Has anyone, by the way, noticed the remarkable likeness Bob has to Bosnian Serb war criminal Radovan Karadjic?) With an icy glare and a slow, monotonous take-no-prisoners delivery, Bob revels in tabloid tantrums. 'Dire', 'Disgrace', 'Shambles', 'Pathetic', 'Plughole', 'Desperate', 'Farce' – this is the vocabulary Bob likes to use. Perhaps I can recommend you play the Bob Willis Game. You can play it at home. In fact, you can play it without leaving the comfort of your sofa. The rules are simple: score one point every time Bob uses one of these words, two points if he talks about 'heads rolling' or 'sackings' or 'chopping blocks', and five points when he inevitably bleats on about the lack of quality English bowlers since . . . well, since him. If you haven't scored over 100 points by tea-time, it's because you dropped off when Paul Allott was on.

What these miserymongers don't appreciate is that we don't want all this maudlin bellyaching. And in any case, that's our job. And our privilege. We're the ones freezing our nuts off at 3.30 a.m. watching England collapse Down Under. We've got a right to moan and grumble. Bob is getting paid handsomely to sit in his shorts quaffing Aussie chardonnay to his heart's content and talk to us about cricket. Sounds a cushy number to me. So what's his problem? We want succour and hope from our commentators.

Reassurance that all is not lost. That maybe this is the day that Ramprakash will get past 29. This is why people like the radio commentary so much. England may be 28 for six but 'Blowers' is on telling you what a lovely, jolly day it is, how the sun is shining, and two red London buses are just going down the Harleyford Road, and an English bobby is cycling home, and oh look, two pigeons are having a spot of 'how's your father' down at long leg. It is a commentary as gooey and sickly as the cream cakes they scoff all day and we absolutely lap it up.

Radio commentary is about painting pictures for the listener, and cricket, with its long pauses in between the moments of action, lends itself perfectly to it. Contrast it, for example, with the verbal epileptic fit that is a radio tennis commentary. Radio's Rembrandt was John Arlott. Blessed with a voice that burred like a distant lawn mower on a summer's afternoon, Arlott's commentary was poetic in its insights. He told us once of a batsman who knows he had just got the faintest of edges to the wicket-keeper and who 'spins on his heel like a boy caught stealing jam'. We've all seen that pained expression tinged with guilt on the face of the erring batsman but it took an artist like Arlott to put it into words.

His retirement was a huge loss but it just spurred Brian Johnston on to even more dottiness. He developed an obsession with the TV soap *Neighbours* and there was a joyous incongruity of listening to Johnners talk in his plummy Eton tones about the trials of Brett and his new girlfriend, or Raylene and her traumatic hysterectomy. Listening to him explain the plot of a particularly gripping episode to that professional Little Englander and cultural snob, Don Mosey, was one of the highlights of the 1988 season.

'Blowers' is a sort of poor man's hybrid of the two. Lacking the poetry of Arlott ('A fluffy white cloud hovers behind

Father Time') and being too studied in his eccentricities (the constant references to buses do rather grate by the third day), he is tolerated rather than revered. He also has an alarming tendency to get facts wrong. Many is the time I have only narrowly avoided a traffic disaster because I turned on the radio to hear 'Blowers' announce the score is 224 for nine when really he meant 229 for four. And he has that maddening habit of getting ahead of himself too: 'That'll be four. That's Thorpe's century. Actually it might not be. It's slowing up on the damp outfield, so there will only be three. Ah no, it's only two. I didn't see Donald down there at third man. Anyway, Thorpe's now on 99. No, 98.'

Christopher Martin-Jenkins and Jonathan Agnew bring a journalistic competence to the box but rarely transcend the mundane. That said they are infinitely preferable to the smugly partial Neville Oliver (when Australia tour) or Tony Cozier (West Indies). We Brits distrust the intentions of foreigners, especially when their countrymen are wiping the floor with us, and if we've got to have our failings aired and picked over, we'd rather it were done by one of us. It took Richie Benaud about ten years to convince us that he was kosher and not sniggering behind Peter West's back and now it is impossible to imagine an English summer without him. My favourite Richie Benaud season was the summer of 1988 when the West Indies toured and brought with them both Roger Harper and Carl Hooper. Both were brilliant fielders who in the one-day series were used to some effect patrolling the covers and the midwicket region stopping innumerable short singles and helping to pressurise the batsmen into something rash. Now, it had long been Richie's practice, ever since the days of Derek Randall, to shout excitedly the fielder's name and that alone when the batsman went for a risky single and a run out was possible. So when England batted you could sit back and giggle contentedly as Richie trilled: 'Hoooopperrrrrr' or 'Haaaarppperrrrrrr' every few overs. Sometimes, if you were really lucky, he would call it wrong and try to correct himself mid-syllable: 'Haaaaarrp-hoooooooperrrrrrrr!' A little more fun went out of cricket the day Roger Harper lost his action and found himself on the sidelines.

The BBC's problem, however, has always been to find a partner for Richie. For many years it was the prosaic Jim Laker, who had a collection of stock phrases he would peddle throughout the day – 'He's gone for the big yahoo.' 'Batsman X didn't trouble the scorers.' 'Y is a useful batsman who can bowl a bit of "seam up on Sundays"', and 'He's gone now' every time a wicket fell. Half an hour of Jim and you were salivating for the puckish and wry Benaud to come back. Following Jim's death, they tried Tony Lewis but you really do need to see the eyebrows to get the full benefit. Latterly, David Gower has been given a shot but sadly, his commentary style lacks the splendour of his batting. But while none of these three could match the dry one-liners or the authoritative analysis Richie offers, they did not make you want to bite your own ears off as much as Jack Bannister.

'In what way does Jack Bannister get on your tits?' is a question that has exercised me, my friend Justin and others down the pub for some years and we have collectively worked up a fairly lengthy discourse on the subject. But Justin has gone one stage further. So concerned is he that he has devised a short questionnaire to enable you to monitor developments.

1. A ball pitches two feet outside leg stump and misses off stump. Would you say:
a) 'That turned a mile.'

b) 'Now that's interesting.'
c) 'Just the slight suggestion of turn there, Geoffrey.'

2. Atherton cuts the ball past point for four. Would you say:
a) 'Lovely shot.'
b) Nothing.
c) 'Atherton cuts the ball past point for four.'

3. Rain has stopped play. Do you:
a) Ask Geoffrey to sum up the play so far.
b) Return viewers back to Des Lynam in the studio.
c) Talk about the Brumbrella (Edgbaston's pitch cover) for half an hour.

4. Who do you believe to be the most potent new-ball attack in the world?
a) Wasim and Waqar.
b) Ambrose and Walsh.
c) Munton and Small.

5. To win friends and get laughs at school, did you:
a) Develop comedy impressions of the teaching staff.
b) Perform elementary magic tricks.
c) Learn to speak while simultaneously breathing out of your nose and then snorting.

If you have answered 'C' to any of these questions you are either Jack Bannister or you are showing signs of becoming just like him. Either way, you should get counselling now.

Justin's revelation that Bannister snorts down the microphone at the end of every sentence was the final straw for me. I increasingly found myself listening out for it. Sometimes I would miss the action because I had my ear pressed against the set trying to get a really good listen to the snort. After a while, all I could think of was the snort.

Sometimes he did it immediately after a sentence. Other times there was a three or four second pause. But there was always an audible snort. Once he went for about 15 seconds without the snort and for a few fleeting moments the gloom in the sitting room lifted and birds chirped merrily again outside as I imagined Bannister had lost the habit. But no such luck. Suddenly, there it came.

I confess it is with some regret that I have felt compelled to share this observation with you because it *will* make Bannister's commentaries all the more unbearable now. But I had to tell someone.

Then there are the summarisers, those old lags earning a Cornhill crust. For many years the BBC used Tom Graveney and Ted Dexter. Tom was a genial old buffer whose approach to summarising was to summarise whatever the commentator had just said. So if Richie said, 'Shot. That'll be four. That's the shot of the day in my book. End of the over. England are 132 for one' (well, it's only an example). Tom would say, 'Well, England are moving along nicely. 132 for one. And in that over we saw a lovely shot. Four from the moment it left the bat.' And this sort of thing would go on all day. The only tricky moment for Tom would be if it rained and all the commentators were rounded up by the eyebrows to talk about things in general and he was asked for his opinion on something before Richie had spoken.

Dexter, however, was free with his opinions and, as you'd expect, most of them were completely hare-brained. One season he became obsessed with players who were 'thin'. But he wasn't talking about the Jonathan Agnews or Sikhander Bakhts of this world. It eventually became clear that he meant players who batted side on and stayed side on in the execution of a stroke. Peter Willey was consequently a 'fat' player. John Carr would today be in the

Cyril Smith category. As we were later to have confirmed on his appointment as chairman of the England committee, Dexter's lunacies were soon to reach new heights.

Peter Parfitt told you exactly what you had just seen for yourself and David Acfield used to talk really, really slowly during the slow-motion replays in the mistaken belief that this would in some way enhance the effect. But for the past decade, we have largely been in the hands of two Yorkshiremen. First, Ray Illingworth and then Geoffrey Boycott. Both have the confidence and authority of never having been wrong in their lives and both are so obsessive about the game that they are nearly always worth listening to.

This confession will come as a shock to some of you who have for your own good reasons developed pathological hatreds of one or both of these Yorkshiremen, but one of the enjoyable facets of following English cricket is the debate and controversy it generates. All over the country, we sit in bars arguing over who should be in the England team, who should be captain, who should be chairman of selectors, etc. and it is the nature, too, of such discussions that cricket fans are very rarely able to agree on any of these matters. In fact, it is my experience that the only thing upon which the entire cricket-following public can agree is that Charles Colvile is a pillock.

Colvile is the man who put the 'W' into TV anchorman and so universally is this accepted that I won't bother to labour the point here. However, I would give credit where it is due to Sky Sports' excellent coverage. OK, I have grave reservations about the make-up of the commentary team, but I can live with that if it means seeing every ball bowled live from New Zealand. Anything beats trying to piece together every third word of a Peter Baxter commentary on a crackly line from Islamabad. Sky has pioneered the use of new technologies. Stump microphones now allow us to hear Alec Stewart shout 'I like it' after every ball. Stumpcam affords us a spectacular view of Graeme Hick being yorked by whichever fast bowler is touring that season. A video marker pen allows Geoff Boycott to play noughts and crosses all over our screens and we now have superslomo and isolated close-up just for good measure. We've come a long way from those days of old when for half the overs in the day all we could see was what looked like a batsman crouched behind Alan Knott's bum.

But, most importantly, the one thing Sky is able to guarantee is we won't be buzzing off to some other sporting event halfway through an over. It is widely accepted that it is impossible to be both a lover of tennis and of cricket. This is partly a legacy from school where you either opted for a man's sport (cricket) or a girlie one (tennis). Every summer for years the tennis set at school, all togged out in their white shorts and Fred Perry tops, would have to run the gauntlet of the changing room with whipped towels raining in on them and cries of 'cissy' ringing in their ears, as we cricketers slipped into our manly flannels. How we laughed as they rubbed their pink thighs and commenced their Françoise Durr impressions on court. But they are the ones laughing now. The television industry being as it is, men from school tennis sets are now in senior positions in the BBC and frankly nothing gives them more pleasure during the Wimbledon fortnight than to cut away to a game of mixed doubles on centre court with England needing one run to avoid the follow-on and Tufnell facing Wasim Akram.

But such gleeful retribution does not stop there. No, one of the consequences of the Birtian BBC's obsession with a rolling news service is that we lose seven minutes of live cricket at the top of each hour. One minute you're watching

Jack Russell dig us out of a hole, the next minute Nicholas Witchell is beaming at you. Old 'ginger nuts' then gives you yesterday's news because it's only noon and nothing's happened yet, and then infuriatingly he gives you the 'latest' Test score which was actually the score two minutes before they left the coverage to give them time to make up the caption. So we find that we have left the cricket to go to the newsroom where within minutes, because there's no news, they start to tell you what was happening in the cricket two minutes before you left the bloody cricket in the first place! At this point all over Britain 'Dear *Points of View*' letters are being composed.

But there is more madness. After the national news we get Penny Tranter on with the national weather with a sun symbol and the words 'Old Trafford' perched over Manchester just in case we had forgotten that the weather was sunny when we were watching the cricket there four minutes ago before we were so rudely interrupted. Then we get the local news and a fascinating story about a hosepipe ban in Catford and then up pops Suzanne Charlton with the local weather. Now, I'm as much a fan of Suzanne as the next man with her big happy smile and sunny (appropriately) personality (though I do think she would endear herself to the whole nation even more if once, just once, when we cut to the weather we find she has brushed all her hair from one side of her head to the other in tribute to her legendary father), but by now it is getting beyond a joke especially when you think that in precisely 53 minutes we'll be going through this whole charade all over again.

It is enough to make you wish it were raining. At least then all these weather bulletins would be of use. We could watch one of those 'hilarious' sequences depicting vignettes of the current Test series the wacky boys in the BBC video editing department put together to the tune of

'Summertime'. Or we could enjoy yet again all misty-eyed a recording of the Ashes series of 1981 with Botham sweeping Ray Bright for his century and Jim Laker commentating as ever with foot fully inserted in mouth: 'What a fine way to go to a six.'

Of course, there are only so many sickies you can throw in a year and various other inconveniences such as weddings, christenings, and summer holidays conspire to deny you access to either TV or radio at critical points in the cricketing calendar. The worst position of all is to be abroad during a Test match. You have to possess a safe-cracker's fingers to find any channel, let alone Radio 4 LW, on most hotel radios and CNN, it would appear, have yet to appoint a Trent Bridge correspondent. Things are a lot better now with mobile phones and understanding people in the office faxing you in your hotel with the score every day, but not so long ago it was not uncommon to find two grown men outside a newstand in Corfu or Majorca fighting over a four-day-old copy of the *Daily Express*. And all just to get the scores and read the match report. If you were really lucky, you might meet someone who had just landed on that day's charter flight from Luton and was fully au fait with the scores. If you were really unlucky, they would then treat you like some long lost friend and you'd end up having dinner with them and then afterwards in the hotel cocktail lounge guarding their Travel Scrabble set while they did a conga around the tables singing the 'Birdie Song'.

Often when on holiday, we try to keep the sense of an English summer at hand by reading one of those ghosted autobiographies of our heroes. These normally have an appalling pun in the title and detail the 'lifestory' of the 22-year-old bowling sensation England have just unearthed and who took 12 wickets on an 'A' tour of Bangladesh last winter. This seems to be a booming business. Darren Gough had played precisely nine Test matches before his book was released, and Dominic Cork had played even fewer before *Uncorked* hit the bookshelves. At this rate we can look forward to reading *County Cork* – the story of Dominic's five-year career with Derbyshire – and *Putting a Cork in it* – Dominic's diary of the tour of India.

With this range of choice, it is essential that you should never allow other people (especially non-cricketing types like wives, girlfriends, mothers, sisters, etc.) to buy a book for you. Too many birthdays have been blighted trying to feign delirium at the receipt of '*Life's A Pitch*' – Harry Brind's hilarious account of the re-laying of The Oval square in 1985 – or pretending that *Shep* – David Shepherd's pop-up book of umpiring hand signals including his famous Nelson hopping routine – is the best Christmas present anyone could have got you. Insist they give you a book token next time.

Back to the match and it is Saturday morning. I am sitting on the sofa with a cushion clamped over each ear. Jack Bannister is on. And England's batting is off. The score is 29 for three with Atherton, Hick and Thorpe all in the pavilion and with Gallian and Stewart nursing broken bones. Only Robin Smith is putting up any resistance to Walsh and Bishop on a perilous pitch. I work out that I have probably watched over 350 days of Test cricket on TV. That's nearly a year of my life. And for maybe a week of that I have had two cushions pressed against each lughole. It is an extraordinarily sad way to spend a week of one's life. But my mind now starts to calculate how many of those 350-odd days were working days – days when either I was skiving at somebody else's expense or at my own, not writing whatever I should have been writing.

I think of all those days with the answering machine

on and then trying to squeeze in a normal day's business between the hours of 1 p.m. and 1.40 p.m. or 3.40 p.m. and 4 p.m. Cricket as a displacement activity certainly has no equal. By the time it's over, the whole day has been displaced and the pubs have just opened. Writing at home in the winter has always been much easier and more productive (unless you were up all night watching Sky and need the days to catch up on your sleep). Of course, there are distractions in winter too. For many years I was a devoted viewer of *Fifteen To One* – a very Thatcherite quiz show which in a neo-Darwinian way has the clever ones picking on the thick ones. I liked it in particular when personal grudges between contestants would develop and Beryl, retired schoolmistress, and Norman, chartered surveyor, would be scrapping it out to the death furiously picking on one another. I also used to watch *Countdown* a lot in the vain hope that one week someone would ask Carol Vorderman for a consonant, a vowel, and two consonants and 'CUNT' would appear on screen. But *Ready, Steady, Cook* is my current favourite even though it is a complete fiddle. The idea is that a well-known chef is given just £5 worth of groceries to produce a slap-up meal. These groceries are allegedly bought at random but always turn out to be the precise ingredients for chicken chasseur. I tell you, it's a con. I don't really watch the programme. I just sit there composing my own list of provisions guaranteed to stump our telly cooks – a pound of sprouts, a tub of ice-cream, some tea bags, and a can of *Pledge*. Now let's see you rustle up a gourmet meal from that lot, chummy. Actually, I'm not sure I would have written much more had I not spent all this time watching cricket, I'd have just watched an awful lot more daytime television.

It's exactly 12.18 p.m. England are all out for 89 and have lost by an innings and 64 runs. It is one of the shortest Test matches in history (only 172.2 overs). Typical. I've put the whole day aside to watch the cricket with no need to field calls from work in a croaky voice, and it's all over. The best alternative it seems *Grandstand* can offer is speedboat racing from Bristol Dock and BBC2 has announced it will be showing *Genevieve* in case you have been out of the country every Easter and Christmas for the last 40 years and missed it.

I suppose I ought to write that script. Yes. I should sit myself down and get writing. But there again, the fridge does need defrosting. Eventually, after I have cleaned the oven, regrouted the bathroom and shampooed the sitting-room carpet, I can find no other distractions. I take the phone off the hook, sit down, and write the first draft. I finish at 5 a.m. on Monday morning and collapse into bed knackered and stinking of household cleaning fluids. At 3.30 p.m. I stagger into work flustered to be greeted by my executive producer with an unfriendly: 'Where the hell have you been? We've been trying to get hold of you all day!'

'Sorry,' I splutter, 'I would have been here this morning, but someone took the bloody batteries out of my alarm clock.'

CHAPTER NINE

Boys with Big Bellies
Middle-aged men
behaving sadly

Micheldever v Acton Casuals

Date: 14 September   *Venue:* Micheldever   *Toss:* Acton

Acton Casuals

M.Devereux	b Guppy	4
R.Wylie	not out	2
C.Cummins	not out	0
Extras		0
Total (1 wicket)		6

Bowling	O	M	R	W
Guppy	2	1	4	1
Bell	1.4	0	2	0

Match Abandoned.

It's 4.20 a.m. and I have just completed my fourth lap of the Wandsworth one-way system. I am driving in sick-stained pyjamas trying to coax one of my daughters off to sleep. If this doesn't work, it'll be her and carrycot on the washer dryer at home where we have found that ten minutes on fast coloureds normally does the trick. The trouble is it risks waking the other one. Since 12.30 a.m. I have gone through our entire repertoire of sleep-inducing stratagems. I have paced up and down the sitting room making gentle sighing noises. I have tried The Cranberries CD on low volume which worked once. And I even showed her a video of *Lillee's Clash with Steele* (video highlights of the 1975 Ashes series) which always makes her mother want her bed, but all to no avail.

I wake with a jolt. How long I have been at these lights I don't know but the good news is that she seems to be asleep. I chuck in another lap just to be sure and psyche myself up for the tricky bit – getting the baby out of the car, through the cool night air, into the house, out of the carrycot and into the night cot without her waking. My stomach knots with tension as I pull up outside the house. A couple of deep breaths and I go for it. Mission accomplished – though there was a dodgy moment when I trod on a fluffy barking toy dog that wouldn't stop yapping and had to be thrown out of the window. Five minutes later I am lying in bed exhausted. It is 4.55 a.m. In just over five hours I am being picked up by my friend, Phil, who has also recently become a father for the first time. Ahead of us is a two-hour drive down the M3 to a village called Micheldever, between Basingstoke and Winchester, a couple of pints in a pub run by the surliest of landlords, and a prompt 2 p.m. start. Never before have I so looked forward to a cricket match – my first match since the twins were born five weeks ago and my first Saturday away from the milk, shit, cry, burp, sick, treadmill – and the joyous prospect of a first-ball duck and a two-hour uninterrupted kip by the boundary.

Phil arrives spot on time. He has the jaunty walk of a free man as he comes up the path.

'How was it?' I enquire. He knows instantly what I'm talking about.

'Down at two, sick at 4.30, sleep at 6.30. You?'

'Aagh. Didn't get them both down until five.'

'God. How many laps?'

'Five.'

Phil gave me the tip about the driving. He reckons he has clocked up over 600 miles in the last few months just trying to get his child off to sleep. Unlike me, though, he prefers not to risk waking the kid up, so he often sleeps in the car with him. The postman taps on the window if they're both still asleep by 7.30.

'What's the weather forecast like?' he asks, turning to the important matters of the day.

'Who cares? If it rains I'm checking into a guest house for the afternoon and sleeping. I am not due back here until 11 and I have no intention of getting back earlier.'

I say my goodbyes to Fran and the girls and we get on our way. Within minutes we are in full male-talk mode. We start as usual by trashing the England cricket team. Phil suffers from a bad case of 'Hickitis' which is a virulent strain of Tourettes Syndrome that is brought on by the inclusion and subsequent poor performance of Graeme Hick in the

England side. To listen to Phil, you would think that the Worcestershire batsman was personally responsible for the systematic deforestation of the Amazon Basin, the outbreak of BSE, and the persecution of Palestinian Arabs and not just a failure to keep out Ambrose's yorkers. Indeed, towards the end of 1995 with back-to-back hundreds against West Indies followed by another hundred in the first Test against South Africa in Pretoria, it looked like Phil's complaint had cleared up. But a string of low scores against India in the first half of 1996 and the familiar sight of his stumps spreadeagled by Waqar, had brought it back with a vengeance. In just one sentence he contrives to question the legitimacy of Mr and Mrs Hick's marriage, cast doubt on his right to British citizenship, and liken his appearance to that of female genitalia. Not bad for an opening salvo on the subject.

I counter with my own hobbyhorse of the time – the selections of Irani and Ealham – and it is but a short hop from there into trashing the latest crop of sitcoms and then on to Euro 96. I am half-way through my compelling treatise on the need to swap McManaman over to the right wing and put Anderton on the left, when Phil points out a woman walking up the Kings Road wearing thigh-length boots and what looks like no more than a chamois leather. We have been on the road for less than ten minutes and we have covered the entire conversational terrain for the day – cricket, TV, football and women. We have both put down certain markers and these will be chewed over at much greater length later but the agenda has been established.

Such conversation is to be further enhanced by the company of Simon, a corporate lawyer, who we are picking up on the way. Phil toots the horn outside Simon's flat and receives a wave from the bedroom window. Two minutes later Simon emerges complete with the enormous coffin in which he carries his never-washed kit, and a girl. She is tall with dark hair and an olive complexion and looks absolutely ravishing to two blokes who have been on starvation rations in the rumpy-pumpy department for some months.

'Hi, fellas. This is Heidi. Can we drop her at Knightsbridge tube?' he booms with the glint in his eye of a man who's been wrapped in clingfilm for long periods of the previous night. Both Phil and I chat politely with Heidi but deep down we are a raging torment of emotions. Heidi's presence confirms to us what every bloke in a relationship suspects: that blokes *not* in a relationship are having more fun. No matter how often you think back to the time when you were single and all those nights on your own eating Kentucky Fried Chicken in front of reruns of *Colditz* on UK Gold, you still believe that all single blokes out there must be playing Twister every night with the girls in Bananarama.

We drop her off. There is a brief display of affection between the two of them outside the car as Phil and I stare blankly ahead, trying to remember how to spell 'sexual intercourse' let alone remember when we last had it. Then Simon jumps back in and we're properly on our way. I watch in the side mirror as Heidi's exquisite body disappears into Harvey Nichols. Phil starts to quiz Simon. We hear all the things we don't want to hear but can't help ourselves from asking the questions. She's 24, an interior designer, dad's got a large pile in Sussex courtesy of a cushy number in the City and she does extraordinary things with chocolate spread. We try desperately to piss on his strawberries.

'So, 24, eh? That's 1973. Good God she won't have heard of Slade,' I carp.

'Or T Rex. Or Wizzard. Or *Starsky and Hutch*,' Phil adds.

Simon shrugs his shoulders. A contented grin wipes across his face as he settles down to catch a few winks sleep.

'I mean what on earth do you talk about with a 24-year-old?' probes Phil further.

'Fellas, do you mind? I didn't get to sleep until six o'clock.'

'Oh, fuck off!!' we cry in unison.

The thing men are most afraid of is settling down. It is a terrifying concept. Settling down leads to buying big houses with big mortgages, and then breeding, and then constantly shelling out hard-earned cash on kids' shoes, bikes, school trips, and going to college. And then you become a grandfather and take up gardening, and then one day you'll be picking your own home-grown runner beans and Bananarama will appear from behind the garden shed and ask if you fancy a game of Twister, and you'll say: 'Thank you but I haven't got time. I've got to get my spuds in and then we're off to Homebase.' That's what we're terrified of becoming. Reaching that point where the idea of a game of Twister with Bananarama doesn't even enter our minds.

Not that for one minute either do we want to become one of those 50-year-olds with a pony tail, or start wearing leather jackets and cowboy boots. Women don't have these problems. Their hormones dictate physically the appropriate stages in life – from the first period, to the need to breed, to the menopause. A bloke doesn't know he's got a mid-life crisis until he finds himself risking bankruptcy to buy a Porsche convertible or cutting out those adverts in the *Evening Standard* that claim to arrest hair loss.

So as we march reluctantly towards 40 contemplating the irony that while hair is sprouting everywhere – on our necks, down our backs, from our ears, our noses, even our arseholes – it is fleeing our scalp quicker than you can say 'Hello, Spamhead', these cricket matches take on an increasing importance. These testosterone-charged days are a means of maintaining links with the hedonism of bachelorhood, distracting us from the travails of impending middle-age, and rekindling those dim and distant fires of our athletic youth.

One of the teams I play for these days is Acton Casuals – a motley crowd of advertising executives and PR johnnies who are all the acquaintances of our captain, and Acton resident, Maurice. Half a dozen fixtures against villages within a couple of hours' drive of London are arranged a year and I try to fit in as many as possible. The standard of play is consistently mediocre but it is the company of men, the male-bonding free from the constraints of political correctness, that we really enjoy.

It is predictable joshing much of the time – expense account girths, receding hairlines, new preppy spectacles, mobile phones, Volvo estates with kiddies' car seats – but it seems to provide countless hours of fun. Battle-lines are constantly redrawn during the course of the day. It could be fatties v the gym boys one minute, single men v married men the next. Then the BMWs v Volvo estates, who then join forces against the 2CVs, who in turn wage war against all those currently being treated for ulcers or other stress-related disorders.

The banter is always competitive and always ruthless and the opportunity to go in for the kill is never declined. I would rather be the gazelle crippled at birth and who struggles to keep up with the rest of the herd being stalked by a leopard than an Acton Casual caught by his teammates wearing a particularly poncey pair of boxer shorts. For the gazelle it is a quick, clean kill. For the Acton Casual, the chances are those boxer shorts will still be being talked about twelve years hence.

One feature of this male camaraderie that I have observed over the years, is the propensity to become involved in 'the pointless challenge'. These can range from the small fry of drinking yards of ale or doing a new beermat trick to trying to break the world record for hopping over 100 metres. All it takes is for somebody to mention idly that the world hopping record for 100 metres is 33.57 seconds and before long someone will pipe up, 'I can beat that.' And another to cry, 'Well, I could beat you.' Five minutes later bodies that were previously conditioned to doing nothing more vigorous than eating pizza while operating a remote control are furiously hopping down one side of a wet outfield. The 33.57 seconds record is never threatened and there is much arguing about whether changing foot constitutes running and the problems of being baulked by competitors in adjoining lanes, as well as references to hopping achievements prior to the cartilage operations that wrecked a promising career in international hopping.

One year during a mid-season get-together in an Acton pub, Trevor, who lived locally, revealed in colloquial fashion that he could find his way back home from the pub blindfold. Within seconds a pedant pounced, a dispute ensued and a wager was struck. Ten minutes later we were all outside while Trevor, who lived three-quarters of a mile away, tried to navigate his safe passage home blindfold and unassisted. The rules decreed that we were only to steer him if his life was in danger. He started well despite a dodgy moment with a tethered dog outside a fish and chip shop but a couple of wrong turnings later he was lost and traipsing round an allotment. Some of us had to leave after 45 minutes of hilarity that saw him crash through strawberry canes and fall in ditches, because we had jobs to go to the following morning, but a quick phone round the next day revealed that he made it home at 2.15 despite crashing into next door's dustbins and waking up the whole street. Still, it was worth it. He had won a tenner and, more importantly, written his name in large letters in the annals of Acton Casuals' Achievements.

You see, a bloke can get older and he can acquire in some cases substantial wealth, power or responsibility, but he never grows up. He could be a large cog in the civil service machine with hundreds of people reporting to him, or a barrister with people's futures in his hands every day, or a City banker making multi-million-pound deals on a daily basis, but that doesn't mean for one minute that he has matured into a wise and considerate human being. Blokes never lose an essential boyishness. Just look at two of our senior politicians as proof. When Major visited South Africa a few years back and took a look at one of the cricket development programmes in a black township, he couldn't wait to slip off his jacket and show off his top spinner. He had that same feeling we all have when we're walking across the park and a football comes rolling towards you. It's all you can do to stop yourself from trapping the ball, going on a mazy dribble around a group of unimpressed nine-year-olds, drawing the keeper, slotting it between two jackets and then running in an arc with your shirt pulled over your head *à la* Ravanelli. And all, obviously, performed to your own David Coleman-style commentary. It is only the presence of your wife and kids that makes you kick the ball helpfully back and proceed undistracted to the picnic zone.

Or remind yourself of Michael Heseltine and practically every one of his successors as Secretary of State for Defence and what do you see? A man responsible for one of the most powerful armies in the world, a leading member of NATO and of the security council of the United Nations, dressed up in a camouflaged flak jacket and being driven around in a Chieftain tank with a big grin all over his face and going Brrrrrrrrrmmmmmmmmmm.

It is the same psychology that we take on to the cricket field. We have observed earlier that cricket is one of the few sports that isolates the individual and his performance from the context of the team. That is to say that unlike most other sports the subordination of the individual to the requirements of the team is not nearly so necessary. Matt Le Tissier, Glenn Hoddle, Alan Hudson, Tony Currie, Stan Bowles *et al.* would all have been able to prosper and retain their unique individual styles much more in a cricket shirt than they were able to in an England football shirt. At village cricket level, however, all this amounts to is a 'Me, me, me charter'. The word 'team' is a veneer in village cricket for eleven blinkered, selfish and thick-skinned blokes stabbing each other in the back, wishing ill-fortune on their colleagues, and mocking their inadequacies. Never be lured into believing that the competitive spirit is limited to a contest between two teams. There is a much grubbier battle going on within your own.

When you are batting in the middle, there is a dirty tricks campaign being waged against you in the pavilion by all those batting below you in the batting order. 'He shouldn't be batting at number 6, he never gets any runs.' 'Aagh! Look at that shot. That should have gone for four. Hit it, man!' 'He hasn't paid his subs yet. Why's a man who still hasn't paid his subs going in at number 6?' Insurrection breaks out between the slips and the wicket-keeper when you're bowling. 'Well, we'll never win now.' 'Why don't we just give them a 25-run head start and save ourselves the trouble of beating around in the bushes looking for the bloody thing?!' And guerrilla warfare is unleashed while you're fielding over at long-on. 'He never buys a round,' says cover. 'He never drives either,' adds mid-off. 'I think priority in the batting should be given to those that pay their way,' moralises cover. 'Or give other people lifts,' concurs mid-off. This biting, sniping and whingeing is going on behind your back all day. And if you doubt it, just think what you're like. When the captain comes up to you and says, 'How about number 6?' do you say: 'Oh, thanks skip, but shouldn't one of the chaps who didn't get a bowl have a chance?' Or do you say: 'No chance of number 5, then?' And then go and raid the team kit for all the best equipment leaving number 5 with a pair of odd gloves, a box with moss growing in it, and a polyarmour bat with about as much 'sweetspot' as a bookshelf. Oh no, you've hidden away the new team bat recently purchased from Lillywhites and you let poor old gloveless number 5 slip on the damp sweaty gloves of the dismissed batsman, a sensation like none other than perhaps conducting an internal examination of a ewe in labour. Depriving him of the decent kit is bad enough, but you then start willing him to get out. You don't want him using up your time and overs. You want to have the time to play yourself in without the pressure of the boundary chorus of 'Get on with it!' that starts about half an hour before tea (the recognised declaration time) and is led by a caucus of numbers 7, 8, 9 who all have a vested interest in promoting wild slogging.

Truth be told only numbers 1, 2 or 3 are allowed to play defensively as a quid pro quo for facing the faster bowlers with a hard ball. But this licence extends only to when the faster bowlers are on. As soon as the medium-paced cannon fodder or the twirlymen come on, the boundary barracking starts as the middle-order twitches with excitement. If the opener ignores these cries, one of the middle-order blokes dons the umpire's coat and gives him out LBW next time the ball hits his pads. It is a cruel world.

The politics of bowling are more subtle. The opening bowlers expect two spells and feel they have a divine right to return at the end to polish off the tail as recompense for bowling at the better batsmen at the beginning of the innings. Second-string bowlers want at least five overs and are livid if 'a batsman who bowls a bit' gets on before they do. Spinners want the end with the long leg-side boundary and see it as an attempt to humiliate them if they don't get it. Nobody wants to bowl when the tattooed bricklayer is in. Everybody wants to bowl at the ten-year-old kid hiding behind his father's pads.

As for fielding, this is the price you have to pay for batting and bowling. Nobody really likes it. Wicket-keeper is the only job worth having but the trade-off is that you normally get to bat no higher than number 7. In a decent club side, the wicket-keeper is the fulcrum of the fielding side constantly motivating his teammates, keeping everyone on their toes. He is also probably the fittest and most athletic player in the team and certainly has the sharpest reflexes. At Acton Casuals level, the wicket-keeper is the bloke who can't bowl, doesn't mind batting in the lower order, and normally does some indispensable job that merits reward like transporting the kit, or buying the match balls. For the rest of us, it is two hours or more of absolute drudgery only made bearable by opportunities for the mockery and scorn of our teammates as they demonstrate a rich and varied repertoire of dropping catches, throwing feebly, diving ponderously, and running breathlessly. It is a simple recipe for hilarity: take 13 players, split into 11 fielders and 2 batsmen, add a small red leather sphere that hurts if it hits you, and enjoy the fun. Balls will be fumbled, missed, kicked over boundaries. Fingers will be bent back, noses will be broken, teeth will be chipped, knees will be cracked. Fielders will lose sight of it, fall over chasing it, career into bushes/fences/other players trying to stop it. All cricketers know that the real pantomime season starts in April and goes through till late September.

Despite the tedium and general loathsomeness of fielding, there is a surprising amount of jockeying for fielding positions as the innings unfolds and there are political undercurrents in practically every one of the captain's decisions. Slip is normally the preserve of your fattest player. He is put there because he is a liability everywhere else. Not since 1987 when he was fielding at fine-leg and the batsman managed an all-run five to a shot to deep square-leg has this butter mountain been allowed to waddle about in the outfield. He has held an actual slip catch on two occasions in just over a decade. Both times the ball was found buried in the HGV Dunlop Radial he calls his midriff. And on another three occasions he has been involved in an 'assist' when a ricochet from one of his chins or his forehead found its way into the wicket-keeper's gloves.

Nobody wants to field at gully. This is 'Casualty Corner' and more broken digits have been claimed by gully than any other position. Anyone who hogged the batting or gave a dubious LBW decision while umpiring should check during the tea interval that his BUPA cover extends to sports injuries for gully is where he's destined. Cover is where the glamour boys field, the budding Jonty Rhodeses or Trevor Penneys of this world who aren't worth their places as batsmen but get the casting vote because of their fielding. Alternatively, this is just the place for the bloke who batted at number 8 and doesn't bowl – keep him involved at cover. Or indeed, the new bloke who scored 74 and you want to suck up to so that he's available for the grudge match against Tubby Turnbull's XI next month.

Mid-off or mid-on is traditionally where the captain fields. Here he offers encouraging words or tips to his bowlers. Alternatively, it is where the chief whinger and heir apparent to the captain wants to stand. Here he can form an unholy alliance with the bowler about the captain's rotten field settings and garner another vote for the end-of-season *coup d'état*.

The boundary is where the fielders with the best throwing arms go. The 'handbag throwers' can't be trusted in the outfield; at least not without the help of Federal Express. It's normally seen as a short straw being put out at third-man or fine-leg – a lonely life away from the cauldron of biting mockery that bubbles out in the middle and long periods of inactivity interrupted by tedious treks over adjacent farmland or forays into deep bramble bushes without the aid of either a flame thrower or sherpa in search of the ball. But then these boundary positions do occasionally have their benefits. One year, the large-breasted new girlfriend of one of our players turned up at the game and, having flicked through the *Mail on Sunday* for a while, suddenly decided to sunbathe topless at a fine third-man position. Within minutes the captain had stationed himself at a very deep fly-slip, long-leg had gone to back stop, deep extra-cover had gone a lot squarer and long-on who felt he was missing out was suggesting he went to fly-gully.

Whether batting, bowling or fielding, it is the lot of the captain to keep a happy ship and impose some sort of collective order on the ten monomaniacs that make up his team. All successful captains have a distinctive quality that separates them from the rest. Illingworth and Brearley were always described as 'shrewd'. Benaud was positive and counter-attacking. Clive Lloyd and Ian Chappell were ruthless. Dermot Reeve was unpredictable. All admirable qualities but pretty irrelevant when confronted with the sort of problems Maurice, and all the other Maurices out there, have to grapple with every weekend. The problems are not tactical but diplomatic: how do you give the man with the Renault Espace, who is crap but brought four players to the ground plus the team kit, two overs without losing the match? Or, as in the case of this match against Micheldever, what to do when you've started one match and a third team turns up all the way from Neasden expecting to play Micheldever as well.

For a while there were some very unhappy faces all round. Eleven blokes from Neasden were livid that they had risked the severing of carnal relations with loved ones by abandoning them for the day to play a cricket match that had apparently been cancelled months ago. Our blokes were concerned that the day was going to be irrevocably disrupted, and the Micheldever captain wanted to hang himself. After much shuttle diplomacy in the Henry Kissinger mould, a plan was hatched to play a triangular tournament in the manner of an Australian summer. Matches of 15 overs a side were played out in what happily turned into a thrilling day's cricket, but it was the sort of test of captaincy Mike Atherton or Mark Taylor never get and it represented one of the few occasions when common sense prevailed over the puerile instincts of your average village cricketer.

As we drive back home in Phil's Range Rover, which has justifiably been the target of much mockery during the day (after all, Phil has had the thing for nearly a year now and has not once required the four-wheel-drive gear despite the rugged terrain that separates his home in Battersea from his office in Kensington), we are generally content with life. We have feasted on sandwiches and sausage rolls and jam scones and Madeira cake – all washed down with strong tea and Flowers Bitter. The face is glowing a little. Must have caught the sun during that vintage innings of 14. The muscles are stiffening up too. Talking of which, Simon is on the phone arranging his rendezvous with Heidi. Phil and I pretend not to listen. But the gist of it seems to be that Heidi is in the jacuzzi sipping a gin and tonic waiting for Simon to get over to her place. Phil and I bridle quietly in the front. When he's finished, I phone home.

'Hello, honey. It's me.' I can hear crying in stereo in the background.

'Where are you?'

'Just coming into London. How has your day been?'

'Hannah has cried since four this afternoon and Polly threw up in the sitting room.'

'Ah, well, don't worry. These things happen.'

'I'm not worrying.' I am beginning to detect a rather hostile tone.

'Good,' I say sympathetically.

'Most of it went over that satellite decoder thing.'

'What?! Does it still work?'

'Pardon?'

'Have you tried it?!'

'No, I haven't had time.'

'Well, look, turn the TV on to number 5 and press "stand by" on the . . .' The phone goes dead. Simon is hooting with laughter in the back seat. Phil is more sympathetic. The biggest row he's ever had with his wife was after an Acton Casuals fixture in Wiltshire. On his way home he decided to get his wife to record the cricket highlights. He phoned from the car and within a few minutes he was deeply involved in giving step-by-step instructions to her on how to operate the VCR. It was like listening to a jumbo jet piloted by a nine-year-old being talked down to a safe landing. However, when he got home he discovered that far from being able to enjoy the BBC's forty-minute cricket compilation she had taped *Aspel and Company* over the 1993 FA Cup final. They rowed and then didn't talk for six days.

But cricket days do not always work out as jolly as today's. We have all had those days when, after a round trip of 150 miles, all you've got to look back on is a first-ball duck out bowled off your forehead trying to reverse sweep their sixth change leg-spinner, a cursory over or two when the match was dead and a bruise between your eyes the size of a tangerine. On such occasions it is important to maintain a sense of humour. To this end, Phil and I spend much of the journey back adding to and refining a dossier of all the lunatics we have come across playing cricket. It is a growing list, for all cricketers have a streak of madness about them and we take comfort from the fact that while we may be considered sad by some, we're not a patch on some of these berks. And so we offer this 'survival guide' to you with our compliments in the hope that our combined thirty years of playing village cricket will benefit some of you as and when you meet these types, as you surely will.

A GUIDE TO VILLAGE CRICKETERS (AND HOW TO DEAL WITH THEM)

1. *THE JOBSWORTH*

This bloke is the one who likes umpiring. He's a stickler for the rules and gets his satisfaction in life from no-balling bowlers, calling 'one short', warning the bowler about running on the pitch even though he's only wearing trainers, and informing batsmen that they had not crossed when the catch was taken, etc.

Tip: Sneak on him to the Inland Revenue. See how he likes chapter and verse of their rule book.

2. *THE JOKER*

The heir apparent to Essex funnyman, Ray East. He bowls with his cap back to front *à la* Boycott, or while smoking a pipe. He uses a pint of beer to mark his run-up, and he's also the one that goes out to bat wearing a kiddies' skateboard helmet.

Tip: Spray Ralgex on his box.

3. *THE ADONIS*
He's 35 and still has a firm, flat stomach, a year-round tan, perfect white teeth and a full head of hair. He's the only one in the team who can still sunbathe in his Speedos without risk of being harpooned and he makes the sexually unfulfilled wives and girlfriends of his teammates writhe with lust on their travel rugs.

Tip: Spread unsavoury rumours concerning him, a hotel in Swanage, and a junior Tory minister.

4. *THE COPYCAT*
When he walks out to bat, he wheels his arms about like Ian Botham or does that silly shuffle Alec Stewart does. And then, when he takes guard, he makes his mark by hammering a bail into the ground like Graham Thorpe. If he's a fast bowler, he insists on bowling two warm-up balls to mid-off who misses them both. If he's a slow bowler, he'll rub his fingers in the footholds between every delivery. Worse still, if he's captain, he'll put his car keys into the wicket before the toss and announce that it will be turning by tea-time.

Tip: Tell him David Gower used to bang his head ten times against the dressing room wall before going out to bat. But at closing time remember to go back to the ground and scrape him off the floor.

5. *GOLDEN BOLLOCKS*
This bloke is as thick as horseshit but makes a fortune running his own antique business and has a gorgeous ex-model of a wife who is into tantric sex. He only plays three or four times a year but always scores a fifty and bowls genuine leg-cutters. Invariably he takes a magnificent catch in the deep or performs a run-out with a direct hit. He is liked by everyone so much that it's not until he and his

Ferrari pull out of the car park that anybody slags him off. He would play a lot more if it weren't for the county squash he plays and the sailing off Cowes in his own yacht he does every July.

Tip: Shag his wife. That'll wipe the smile off his face. And maybe put one on yours.

6. *BIFFO*

The traditionalist in the team (and quite probably the captain). He prefers the cream fifties-style flannels to the modern nylon variety and wears canvas boots complete with steel toe caps and a psychedelic cap as worn by C.P.Mead. But it is perhaps more in the *way* he likes cricket to be played that he really shows his true colours. He abhors flashy stroke players or bowlers who 'mix it up'. 'Line and length' is his mantra. But real joy, perversely, comes not from winning but in an honourable draw secured in fading light with a batting performance from numbers 8 and 9 reminiscent of Mafeking.

Tip: Tell him Alec Bedser wouldn't get in the England side today and enjoy the spluttering tantrum.

7. *TRIGGER*

Reveals himself when umpiring. He is either completely ignorant of the LBW law and makes his decision on random criteria like the quality of the appeal in terms of its instantaneous orchestration (technical merit) and level of histrionics (artistic impression). Or he has an elephantine memory for past perceived injustices and hasn't forgotten that decision you made against him in 1987.

Tip: Shoot him. (Before somebody else does.)

8. *ROY ROGERS*

Opposite of the above. If you fell on the ball as it was rolling towards the stumps, 'Roy' would still not give you out on the basis that he could not be sure it was going to hit. Maybe a freak hurricane would have blown the ball off course. Or perhaps Martians would land and confiscate the ball. You never know. That's why he always gives the batsman (his own teammates) the benefit of the doubt.

Tip: Employ a personal bodyguard for him or you may find when you leave the bar that the opposition have impaled him on a bollard in the car park.

9. *WALTER MITTY*
'Having trouble with the arm ball, Skip,' as another sails out of the ground. Or, 'You had to be a good player to get a nick on that one,' as he returns to the pavilion caught behind hanging his bat out to dry. And then in the pavilion, 'My batting technique is more suited to the bouncy pitches of Australia.'

Tip: Start fundraising to send him there.

10. *THE SKINFLINT*
Hasn't bought a round since the Suez crisis, he drinks halves when other people are buying in the hope they won't remember and is never staying but always on the verge of leaving. Splashed out on a pair of Tony Greig batting mittens in 1975 and though they now look like a pair of grubby oven gloves, he won't be parted from them. He still uses a Slazenger bat with the trademark green stripes on the splice as used by Alan Knott and others from the early seventies.

Tip: Steal his wallet and enjoy watching a grown man cry.

I drag my weary body and heavy kitbag out of Phil's car and watch him pull off before turning to the house and preparing to face the music. The light in our bedroom is on, and mercifully, I can't hear any crying. As I walk up the garden path, I spot the fluffy barking toy dog I threw out of the window last night. I pick it up and give it a little squeeze but it has lost its bark. I only hope Fran has too.

CHAPTER TEN

Fantasy Island
A glimpse of the future

England v Australia (4th Test)

Date: 20 July 2001   *Venue:* Trent Bridge   *Toss:* England

England

M.A.Atherton	lbw b McGrath	104
† A.J.Stewart	c&b Fleming	51
N.V.Knight	c Bevan b Fleming	13
G.P.Thorpe	c Healy b Julian	276
J.P.Crawley	run out	84
A.D.Brown	c Healy b McGrath	93
* A.J.Hollioake	not out	64
A.F.Giles	not out	24
D.G.Cork		
D. Gough		
R.B.Croft		
Extras		31
Total (6 wickets declared)		710

Bowling	O	M	R	W
McGrath	31	4	121	2
Fleming	33	2	133	1
Julian	27	3	101	2
Warne	40	4	209	0
Blewett	11	4	40	0
Bevan	18	2	73	0
Waugh	4	0	33	0

Australia

* M.A.Taylor	b Cork	6	c Atherton b Giles	0
M.J.Slater	lbw b Gough	9	c Crawley b Croft	4
R.T.Ponting	c Giles b Gough	0	b Giles	7
M.E.Waugh	b Gough	1	c & b Giles	10
M.G.Bevan	c Stewart b Cork	0	st Stewart b Croft	9
G.S.Blewett	c Stewart b Cork	0	c Hollioake b Giles	8
† I.A.Healy	st Stewart b Croft	17	c Stewart b Croft	3
B.P.Julian	lbw b Hollioake	19	not out	21
S.K.Warne	c Cork b Hollioake	0	b Croft	0
D.W.Fleming	lbw b Gough	4	c Knight b Croft	1
G.D.McGrath	not out	4	c Brown b Giles	4
Extras		3	Extras	14
Total		63	**Total**	81

Bowling	O	M	R	W	O	M	R	W
Gough	11.3	3	15	4				
Cork	9	1	21	3				
Hollioake	8	1	17	2				
Croft	4	2	7	1	18	6	37	5
Giles	1	1	0	0	17.4	4	30	5

England won by an innings and 566 runs.

England completed an emphatic victory midway through the morning session of the fourth day to go 4–0 up in the series and win the Ashes for the first time since Mike Gatting's triumphant tour Down Under in 1986–87. A quarter of a century of Australia's hegemony in these contests was ended when McGrath was caught in the leg trap off the bowling of Giles to give the Warwickshire all-rounder a second-innings five-wicket haul for the third time in the series. He and his spin twin Croft bowled unchanged and ripped through the Australian line-up as the ball turned prodigiously on a dusty pitch.

None of the Australian batsmen was able to cope with the spinners in the same way that they failed in humid conditions on Saturday evening when the ball was swinging for Cork and Gough. Australia were routed in both innings – the first time they had failed to reach three figures twice in the same match and this was their heaviest defeat in Test history.

England captain Adam Hollioake stood on the pavilion balcony and held aloft the replica urn to an ecstatic crowd that had spilled on to the outfield and were revelling in the party atmosphere. It was a sweet moment too for those former captains and old warhorses, Alec Stewart and Mike Atherton, who had been at the receiving end of so many Ashes encounters over the years. Hollioake ushered them forward to receive the plaudits of the crowd for their past efforts and for the reaching of personal landmarks during this match. Atherton in scoring his 23rd century finally broke Graham Gooch's record Test aggregate of runs and Alec Stewart became only the third England wicket-keeper to take 200 dismissals which, allied to his 7,000-odd runs, must make him the greatest wicket-keeper/batsman of all time.

The fate of the Ashes was never in doubt once England had amassed such a mammoth total. The centrepiece of the innings was Thorpe's magnificent 276 (9 sixes, 38 fours) which occupied 557 minutes and provided a platform for the other English batsmen to play their shots. Having failed to convert fifties into hundreds for so long in his career, this was the third double hundred in his last ten innings and puts him in the pantheon of great English batsmen.

Once Atherton and Stewart had given England a solid start, Thorpe, Crawley, Brown and Hollioake were all able to tuck into the bedraggled Australian attack. Warne, who had a wretched match, was savagely treated by all the English batsmen who seemed intent on wreaking revenge for the many failures against him in the past. The balding leg-spinner has looked overweight and short of breath through much of this tour and there have to be doubts about him visiting these shores again as a Test player. Without Warne's usual potency, the rest of Australia's bowling looked predictable and pedestrian.

As for the batting, Taylor and Slater who have so often been a thorn in England's flesh now look past their sell-by date, while Ponting, Bevan and Blewett just don't seem to have the stomach for a fight when things go against them. The once majestic Waugh is a shadow of his former self as doubts remain as to whether he will ever adjust properly to contact lenses. Even that redoubtable fighter Healy was unable to marshall resistance against a rampant England that have thoroughly outplayed their opponents in all four Tests this summer.

England coach Dermot Reeve declared the team's intention to secure a 6–0 whitewash and looked forward with chairman of selectors Mike Brearley to a five-Test series against Sri Lanka in what now represents a world championship decider. Graham Thorpe received the Man of the Match award from ECB president Lord Major of Foster's Oval.

My God, I feel better for that. Who needs a mud bath with Claudia Schiffer when you can read that to yourself? It's laced with a decade of pain that report. But does this fantasy have any chance of becoming a reality? Is this sort of strutting and ruthless performance ever achievable by an England side?

Already, the lovely warm fantasy of a few lines ago is being subsumed by dark, nightmarish thoughts. I see Charles Colvile hosting *Grandstand* and talking to England's chairman of selectors, Derek Pringle. He is trying to explain away England's humiliating whitewash at the hands of Papua New Guinea. 'Do you have any regrets about recalling Gooch and Gatting to the side aged 49 and 45 respectively?' asks Colvile. 'No. They both topped the county averages last season. They are probably still the best batsmen in England,' retorts Pringle.

Then we leave the studio to go to live cricket. But it is raining. Jack Bannister is talking about how nice and sunny it is in South Africa. Richie Benaud has no face, just this enormous eye staring back at you and Tony Lewis has backcombed his eyebrows over his bald pate. We cut to a scorecard. England are 44 for six against Liechtenstein. Aaaaaaaarrrgh!!

More frightening, perhaps, is the thought that I will be nearly 40 in 2001. Already there are increasing signs (not least around my waist) that I am about to join that sad band of men – the middle-aged cricketer. Last year I made my debut for a friend's team and was asked by their captain if I fancied doing first slip – the fatties' position. I was shocked to realise that my credentials as a swooping Randallesque cover point were no longer obvious. And last year also saw my dismissal by the thirteen-year-old son of another friend of mine with what he claimed was a googly. It seemed only yesterday he was trying to kill his baby sister by repeatedly banging her on the head with a Tonka toy, and the next minute he is explaining the ramifications of a common European currency to me and bowling unplayable leg-breaks.

Growing old is awful. Realising that you are is even worse. I've started unplugging the television at night – something I have never done before. I realise I am slowly turning into my father. Soon I'll be checking for cold spots on the radiators and cutting out articles in the personal money supplements about pensions. I don't do any exercise in the winter. I've joined a gym but have only been three times in nine months. That's £87.33 a visit. I could have had a bloody good blow-out for that. I gave up batting in nets years ago because I couldn't see the bowlers let alone the ball under the artificial lights at The Oval, but now I'm contemplating giving up the bowling as well. Last week I went for the first net of the season and bowled gentle off-spin for an hour followed by vigorous drinking of beer with vodka chasers for two hours. I woke up at 4 a.m. on the sofa in torn jeans and cuts on my knees plus a splitting headache. How I got into this state I have no idea but I won't be bowling in the nets again in a hurry. It's too dangerous. I'll just go for the drinks next time.

Another season beckons. There will be the regular fixtures with the Casuals and three or four with Anabasis CC (n.b.

Greek for an upcountry campaign) run by the Clarke Bros.
– Giles, Nigel and Matt. This year Giles, who's made a lot of
money in pets and proved that 'where there's muck, there's
pets', has acquired the ultimate toy for a boy – his own cricket
pitch. The wicket is being prepared by the Lords groundsman
Mick Hunt, and already this fixture down in Wiltshire looks
to be a highlight of the coming season. In fact, just thinking of
the season ahead lures me into a fantasy world of me scoring
impish half-centuries and snaffling five-wicket hauls.

I am in the middle of one of these daydreams when Fran's
voice penetrates through the soft-focus scene of me on a
glorious summer's day hitting the church spire at Frieth for
yet another six.

'Who is Jim Foat?' enquires Fran.

'What?' I splutter, taken aback.

'The girls yesterday kept pointing to the bloke in the deli
and saying "Jim Foat, Jim Foat".'

'Well, maybe that's his name. Maybe someone told
them.'

'No. His name is Neil. They said he looked like Jim Foat.
You had shown them a photo.'

'Me?'

'Yes.'

Well, I didn't want her to know I'd been showing them
my *Wisdens*, did I? So, I lied. 'Oh, I think he might be a
character in that *Postman Pat* video.'

'Really?'

'Yes.'

'That's odd. Because they said you told them he was a
crap Gloucestershire batsman of the early seventies.'

'Ah.'

'I do wish you wouldn't use the word "crap" in front
of them.'

'Well, it's true.'

I Think I'll Manage

George Sik

'This is a cracking book . . . Sik gets inside the mind of the modern manager and makes the tight-lipped fellas open up far more than usual' *Goal*

Fantasy Football has made would-be managers of us all, but do we really know what the job entails? Football management is one of the most stressful jobs in the country – and one of the most intriguing. How *do* the various managers differ in their approaches and deal with the pressure? What is it about a manager's personality that can spell success or failure? Here leading psychologist George Sik puts football management under the microscope in a revealing yet brilliantly entertaining and humorous look behind the scenes. Over the course of a season, he was given many fascinating insights by some of the best-known names in the game, including:

Dave Bassett • Tommy Burns • Joe Kinnear • Mark McGhee • Alan Smith • Jim Smith • Walter Smith • Terry Venables

Combining empathy, wit, and the kind of curiosity only a die-hard football fan possesses, George Sik reveals more about how managers do their job in this remarkable book than any other that has been published.

'A feature of the book is the honesty and depth of the responses . . . The managers open up in a way they never would with journalists. Unsurpassable.' *Total Football*

'A fascinating subject' *Sunday Times*

NON-FICTION / SPORT 0 7472 5294 7

Kicking in the Wind

Derick Allsop

'If someone is buying you a sports book, ask for
Kicking in the Wind' Evening Standard

There is another kind of football life, light years
away from the fame and riches of the
Premiership, where the challenge is survival
rather than glory. This is the reality and drama of
a typical small-town football club.

Kicking in the Wind is a fly-on-the-wall account of
a year in the life of Rochdale FC, a club that has
the longest unbroken run in the bottom division
of the English league. With unprecedented access
to all areas, Derick Allsop takes the reader on the
team bus, onto the bench, and into the changing
room and boardroom. The result is a soap opera
that uniquely captures the hope and despair,
humour and conflict, both on stage and behind
the scenes.

Following the cash-strapped club through a
typically rollercoaster season, *Kicking in the Wind*
is a candid and uncensored depiction of life in
soccer's bargain basement which gets closer to the
reality than any other account published.

'Well worth reading'
When Saturday Comes

NON-FICTION / SPORT 0 7472 5641 1